JAN 8 6 6 6 22 · 35

A Basic
Grammar
of
Modern English

second edition ━━━━━━━

A Basic Grammar of Modern English

Bruce L. Liles
University of Missouri—St. Louis

PRENTICE–HALL INC., Englewood Cliffs, New Jersey 07632

Library of Congress Cataloging-in-Publication Data

Liles, Bruce L.
  A basic grammar of modern English.

  Includes index.
    1. English language—Grammar—1950–   . I. Title.
PE1106.L497 1987   428.2   86-9304
ISBN 0-13-061870-5

Editorial/production supervision and
  interior design by **Lisa Halttunen**
Cover design by **Photo Plus Art**
Manufacturing buyer: **Ray Keating**

PRINTED IN THE UNITED STATES OF AMERICA

10 9 8 7 6 5 4 3 2 1

ISBN 0-13-061870-5   01

PRENTICE-HALL INTERNATIONAL (UK) LIMITED, *London*
PRENTICE-HALL OF AUSTRALIA PTY. LIMITED, *Sydney*
PRENTICE-HALL CANADA INC., *Toronto*
PRENTICE-HALL HISPANOAMERICANA, S.A., *Mexico*
PRENTICE-HALL OF INDIA PRIVATE LIMITED, *New Delhi*
PRENTICE-HALL OF JAPAN, INC., *Tokyo*
PRENTICE-HALL OF SOUTHEAST ASIA PTE. LTD., *Singapore*
EDITORA PRENTICE-HALL DO BRASIL, LTDA., *Rio de Janeiro*
WHITEHALL BOOKS LIMITED, *Wellington, New Zealand*

Contents

Preface   ix

chapter 1
Subjects, Predicates, and Objects   1

  Subjects and Predicates   3
  Direct Objects   8
  Adverbs and Adverbial Nouns   13
  Prepositions and Particles   15
  Indirect Objects   18
  Summary   21
  Exercises   21

chapter 2
Complements and Appositives   24

  Subjective Complements   24
  Appositives   30

Objective Complements | 33
Adverbial Complements | 33
Questions | 36
Exercises | 37

chapter 3
The Verb Phrase | 40

Past Tense | 41
Present Tense | 44
Future Tense | 46
Progressive Tenses | 48
Perfect Tenses | 49
Present Progressive Tenses | 51
Mood | 53
Summary | 56
Exercises | 57

chapter 4
Passives | 61

Passives with *Be* | 61
Past Participles and Adjectives | 67
Passives with *Get* | 68
Why Use the Passive? | 71
Exercises | 74

chapter 5
The Noun Phrase | 77

Unique Nouns and Names of Classes | 78
Possessives | 81
Adjectives | 86
Compounds | 89
Exercises | 91

chapter 6
Clauses and Phrases That Modify Nouns   94

Relative Clauses	95
Participial Phrases	100
Adverbials	105
Restrictive and Nonrestrictive Modifiers	105
Exercises	111

chapter 7
Phrases and Clauses as Noun Phrases   116

Noun Clauses	117
Gerund Phrases	124
Infinitive Phrases	129
Phrases, Clauses, and Sentences	131
Exercises	134

chapter 8
Movable Modifiers   138

Adverb Clauses	140
Absolute Phrases	142
Infinitive Phrases as Adverbials	143
Fronted Noun Modifiers	145
Extraposed Noun Modifiers	146
The Placement of Modifiers	148
Exercises	153

chapter 9
Compounding   156

Coordinating Conjunctions and Conjunctive Adverbs	159
Punctuation of Compound Sentences	163
Other Compound Structures	164

Parallel Structure   166
The Order of Conjoined Elements   167
Compounding and Subject–Verb
    Agreement   168
Exercises   171

chapter 10
Pronouns   176

Pronouns and Their Antecedents   177
Intensive and Reflexive Pronouns   182
Pronoun Case Forms   186
Standards of Usage   193
Exercises   197

chapter 11
Sentence Structure and Complexity   201

Disruption of the SVO Order   203
Embedded Sentences   205
Interruptions   207
Hemingway and Conrad   209
Exercises   212

Appendix: Parts of Speech   215

Nouns   217
Pronouns   219
Verbs   221
Adjectives   223
Adverbs   227
Prepositions   229
Conjunctions   231
Interjections   232
Conclusion   232
Exercises   233

Index   235

Preface

This book is designed for those students whose primary interest is learning about the structures of written English rather than the methodology of a particular grammatical model. Consequently, there are no discussions of the goals of the traditionalists, structuralists, tagmemicists, stratificationalists, generative-transformationalists, Neo-Firthians, or others who have made important contributions of the study of language during this century. Each chapter describes some aspect of English, and the discussions are drawn eclectically from various grammatical models.

The book includes topics ranging from simple sentence structures to the more complex. It begins with the Subject–Verb–Object structure and proceeds to show how it may be expanded with optional adverbials, auxiliary verbs, and various kinds of modifiers. Finally, such structures as noun clauses, gerund and infinitive phrases, and compound constructions are considered. In addition to providing descriptions of these structures, the book tries to explain why we use them and why one arrangement may be better than another. Although the book has deliberately been kept short, the most important structures in English are included, most of them in some detail.

It is assumed that the users of this book have a dual interest: to learn about English sentence structure and to acquire enough knowledge to enable them to apply this material. Some will be interested in studying grammar as an aid to understanding literature and as a tool for analyzing style. Others will study it for its applications to their writing or to the teaching of reading and composition. Still others who are planning to study linguistics as a discipline in itself need an understanding of the structure of English as background for more advanced work. Throughout, it is assumed that the readers have a dual interest, not just a desire to learn grammar for itself.

The structure of the second edition is basically the same as that of the first. The first three chapters have been rewritten as two chapters to provide for better organization of the basic sentence elements. In these chapters, new material has been added on adverbial nouns, verb–particle combinations, deleted objects, and adverbial complements. Many of the topics covered in the first edition have been expanded. In Chapter 3, "The Verb Phrase," the section on tense has been rewritten to provide a fuller explanation of the relationship between tense and time. There is also a new section on mood in this chapter. The remaining chapters have been revised less extensively than the first three, but most of them contain sections that have been added or rewritten.

I would like to thank my colleagues both at UMSL and elsewhere who have offered suggestions for improving the first edition of this book. In particular, I appreciate the comments from the following reviewers selected by Prentice-Hall: Wanella Huddleston, Western Kentucky University; Willie E. Page, Jr., West Chester University; Twila Yates Papay, Hofstra University; Royal Skousen, Brigham Young University; Eugene Smith, University of Washington, Seattle. Most of all, I want to thank my students.

Bruce L. Liles
St. Louis

A Basic
Grammar
of
Modern English

chapter 1 ═══════════

Subjects, Predicates, and Objects

To the average person, no single element of language is more noticeable than the word. When confronted with a mumbling speaker or poor acoustic conditions, we react with, "I couldn't understand a word." We do not say, "I couldn't understand a sentence," or comment on the unintelligibility of the phrases, clauses, or syllables.

There are various reasons for our being more conscious of words than of other elements of language. In our own speech and writing, we sometimes grope for words, or we wonder whether we are using a given term properly. We never experience a mental block for an entire sentence the way we do for a word, nor do we look sentences up in a dictionary. If we play scrabble or work a crossword puzzle, we find ourselves again searching for words, not for sentences or clauses.

We are also aware of the words that other people use. As we try to listen to a speaker talk about *epenthesis, metathesis,* and *apocope,* we realize that our unfamiliarity with the words is a hindrance to understanding the lecture. At other times we may notice that someone is using terms different from those we normally use, for example calling a carbonated beverage a bottle of *pop* when we use some other name, such as *soda, soft drink,* or *cold drink.*

Or we may question the appropriateness of a given word for some occasion. We would not be very sympathetic if we told a widow that we were sorry her husband had *croaked.* Some words do not belong to casual conversations about trivial subjects (*felicitous, salutary, enigmatic, multifarious*); others are more appropriate for conversation than for formal writing (*tacky, a dump, awful, flaky, tickled, to goof*). If a person has had too much to drink, we may refer to him or her as being *inebriated, intoxicated, drunk, plastered, polluted, soused,* and so on. These terms do not differ in meaning, but their use is restricted to appropriate contexts. Words stand out when they are either too stiff or too casual for the occasion.

Such examples as these are familiar to all of us, and they tend to make us think that language is nothing more than words. Yet there are other times when we discover that just a knowledge of words is not enough. For example, we recognize such words as *kangaroo, tourist,* and *chase* as having meanings that can be stated in a dictionary. When combined, these words take on additional meanings, depending upon how they relate to one another:

> **1.1** The tourist chased the kangaroo.
>
> **1.2** The kangaroo chased the tourist.

The arrangement shows whether the tourist or the kangaroo performed the act and which one was affected by it. Since we normally use words in sentences rather than by themselves, sentence structure is as important to language as words are.

For another example, every child in kindergarten knows the meanings of *I, me,* and *myself;* it is, therefore, not unfamiliarity with the meanings of these words that causes many adults to hesitate over the following choice:

> **1.3a** There was no one there but Constance and *me.*
>
> **b** There was no one there but Constance and *I.*
>
> **c** There was no one there but Constance and *myself.*

In this particular instance, careful speakers and writers use the first version, *Constance and me,* since *me* is object of the preposition *but;* in others they select one of the other options:

    1.4   He knew that Constance and *I* were responsible.

    1.5   I bought it for Constance and *myself*.

They select *I* in **1.4** because it is a subject and *myself* in **1.5** because *I* precedes it in the same clause. It is the sentence structure that determines which pronoun (*I*, *me*, or *myself*) we use, not the meanings of words.

SUBJECTS AND PREDICATES

Words in a sentence may relate to one another in several ways. One of these is compounding: *bread and butter, a knife or a fork, not Rachel but Eloise*. Or we may use certain words to modify others, as when we add adjectives to *a tree* to tell what kind it is: *a tall tree, a stately tree*. Sometimes we let words cluster together in a phrase: *over the house, near the highway, beside Judy*. All of these relationships are found frequently, but one occurs more often than any of the others: the subject and predicate relationship. Because it is found in every sentence, we are starting our study with it.

    Several definitions have been suggested for the subject, but none of them is very satisfactory. At times the subject is the one that performs an action, as shown by the italicized words below:

    1.6   *The repairman* knocked.

    1.7   *A woman* ran.

    1.8   *Those people* laughed.

But in other sentences the subject is the receiver of the action:

    1.9   *The curtain* tore.

   1.10   *The glass* broke.

At other times it is the person or thing that is described:

   1.11   *Larry* looked bored.

   1.12   *Your cousins* resemble each other.

In still other sentences it is difficult to state how the subject relates to the predicate in meaning:

1.13 *It* is snowing.

1.14 *Carol* is likely to be late.

1.15 *The medicine* was hard to swallow.

In **1.13** *it* has no real meaning. In **1.14** we are not saying that *Carol* is likely; rather, it is the entire proposition *that Carol will be late* that is likely. Similarly, we are not saying that the medicine was hard in **1.15**. Any attempt to define the subject on the basis of meaning is frustrating.

Some people have suggested that we can recognize subjects by asking "Who?" or "What?" as in these sentences:

1.16a Sandra jumped.

b *Who* jumped?

1.17a The mattress fell.

b *What* fell?

To follow this test, we have to know what the subject is from the start, because an alternate direction would be, "Replace the subject with *who* or *what*." Not only must we have already recognized the subject before we perform this operation; we have to know whether it names a human or not because we use *who* for humans and *what* for nonhumans. We knew, for example, to use *who* in **1.16** and *what* in **1.17**.

The most useful means of learning to recognize subjects is through examples. With only the twelve sentences we have examined so far (**1.6–1.17**), you should have no difficulty finding the subjects in the following sentences:

1.18 This shirt shrank.

1.19 His houses burned.

1.20 A man laughed.

1.21 Lucy groaned.

Wherever possible, we will avoid definitions and use examples instead.

The words following the subject are called the **predicate**, as shown by the italicized words below:

1.22 Harriet *coughed*.

1.23 The car *crashed*.

A predicate may consist of just a verb, as in these sentences (*coughed* and *crashed*), but there is usually more, as we shall see in the sections that follow.

In examining subjects and predicates, we should notice three features of their combination. First, we are not free to arrange them in any order that we choose. The subject normally precedes the predicate:

> **1.24a**   The flower drooped.
> **b** *Drooped the flower.

The asterisk means that **1.24b** is not a possible English sentence. Although we may find similar sentences in earlier poetry, for present-day English **1.24b** is not possible. In later chapters we will see that this order is sometimes altered, such as in questions and a few other structures. However, we recognize the usual position for the subject as that before the predicate.

Second, when the verb is in the present tense, it often changes in form, depending upon whether the subject is singular or plural:

> **1.25a**   Your shoe *squeaks*.
> **b**   Your shoes *squeak*.

When the singular *shoe* is the subject, the verb ends in *-s: squeaks*. For the plural *shoes*, there is no ending on the verb. Agreement of subject and verb in English is usually restricted to the present tense. In the past there is no change:

> **1.26a**   Your shoe *squeaked*.
> **b**   Your shoes *squeaked*.

One verb is exceptional in that it shows agreement in both present and past tense. This is the verb *to be*, which has the present-tense forms *am, is,* and *are* and the past forms *was* and *were:*

> **1.27a**   I *am* here.
> **b**   The package *is* here.
> **c**   The packages *are* here.
> **d**   The package *was* here.
> **e**   The packages *were* here.

In the past tense we distinguish between *was* and *were*, according to whether the subject is singular or plural.

In addition to word order and subject-verb agreement, we recognize restrictions regarding which subjects may occur with certain verbs. For example, sentences **1.28–1.30** are possible, but **1.31–1.33** are not:

> **1.28**   The referee yelled.
>
> **1.29**   A diver yelled.
>
> **1.30**   We yelled.
>
> **1.31**   *The cup yelled.
>
> **1.32**   *The geranium yelled.
>
> **1.33**   *The worm yelled.

Only names of humans or a few animals may be the subject of *yell*. Some verbs permit only subjects that are concrete (*fall, jump*); some take subjects pertaining to time (*elapse*); and others have still further restrictions.

When a sentence is short and uncomplicated, you can recognize the subject and predicate easily. But even with short sentences, there are features that may cause problems: elements coming between the subject and predicate and inverted order.

When a prepositional phrase is placed between the subject and verb, there may be a tendency to mistake the object of the preposition for the subject:

> **1.34a**   The carpet in this room is dusty.

If you mark off the prepositional phrase, you will find the sentence easier to analyze:

> **1.34b**   The carpet [in this room] is dusty.

Carpet, not *room*, is the subject. In sentences such as this one, you may appeal to meaning by asking what is dusty, the carpet or the room. For other sentences, however, meaning alone is not very helpful.

> **1.35**   *One* [of my teeth] is loose.
>
> **1.36**   *Some* [of the windows] are dirty.
>
> **1.37**   *All* [of the shoes] need polishing.

In sentence **1.35**, you may argue that it is only *one* that is loose, not all *my teeth;* in **1.36**, only *some* are dirty, not all *the windows*. Such reasoning is useless for **1.37**, where *the shoes* could be said to need polishing as much as *all* do, yet the subject is *all*, not *shoes*. Subjects are determined by sentence structure, not meaning.

The following pairs of sentences show how sentence structure rather than meaning can be used to recognize subjects:

1.38a   Several *members* left early.

   b   *Several* [of the members] left early.

1.39a   Three *birds* flew away.

   b   *Three* [of the birds] flew away.

1.40a   All the *money* is counterfeit.

   b   *All* [of the money] is counterfeit.

If you mentally mark off all prepositional phrases, you will not mistake an object of a preposition for a subject. A subject cannot be part of a prepositional phrase. You may find it useful to mark these phrases with a pencil until you are able to locate them with ease.

The second structure that sometimes causes problems in locating subjects is inverted order. The normal order is subject, then verb, then adverb or prepositional phrase:

1.41   The flowers are outside.

1.42   Dandelions grew in the yard.

Occasionally this order is inverted so that the adverb or prepositional phrase comes first, followed by the verb, then the subject:

1.43a   Next comes the *conclusion*.

1.44a   Into the traffic rolled the *ball*.

Sentences like these are easier to work with if you convert them into normal order:

1.43b   The *conclusion* comes next.

1.44b   The *ball* rolled into the traffic.

If you mark off the prepositional phrase in **1.44a**, you notice that there is nothing before the verb that can be the subject.

Sentences starting with *there* are always in inverted order.

When *there* is used merely as a filler for the subject position rather than as an adverb of place, it is called an **expletive**.

> **1.45** *There* was an unpleasant odor in the room. (expletive)
>
> **1.46** I stood *there*. (adverb of place)

You can usually rearrange sentences with *there* into those with normal order by deleting the expletive and rearranging the elements:

> **1.47a** There is a *wasp* in the room.
>
> **b** A *wasp* is in the room.
>
> **1.48a** There is *someone* at the door.
>
> **b** *Someone* is at the door.
>
> **1.49a** There were many *people* at the convention.
>
> **b** Many *people* were at the convention.

As you progress to more complicated sentences, you will find a few for which rearrangement is not possible:

> **1.50a** There are some *sentences* that cannot be arranged.
>
> **b** *Some *sentences* that cannot be rearranged are.

When you reach sentences like this one, you will be accustomed to looking for the subject after the verb.

DIRECT OBJECTS

Most of the sentences examined so far have contained only a verb in the predicate. There are other sentences that are not complete with just a verb:

> **1.51a** *The woodcarver shut.
>
> **1.52a** *Herbie insulted.
>
> **1.53a** *The hammer hit.

Something else is needed:

> **1.51b** The woodcarver shut *the door*.

1.52b Herbie insulted *the passengers*.

1.53b The hammer hit *the woman*.

The structure following the verb in each of these sentences is called a **direct object**. The predicate in each case consists of the verb and whatever follows it: *shut the door, insulted the passengers, hit the woman*.

The direct object is sometimes defined as the receiver of the action or the person or thing directly affected by it. For some sentences this definition is acceptable:

1.54 Tom chased *me*.

1.55 The teacher slapped *the student*.

1.56 Lucille threw *the eraser*.

For other sentences the object neither receives action nor is affected in any way:

1.57 Charles missed *the plane*.

1.58 The witch saw *the moon*.

1.59 Beth turned *the corner*.

1.60 The moths ate *a hole* in my coat.

Nothing happened to the plane, moon, or corner in **1.57–1.59**, nor in **1.60** do we mean that the moths were stupid enough to eat a hole instead of woolen fabric.

It has been suggested that the question words *what* and *whom* be used to locate direct objects:

1.61a Mark nodded his head.

  b Mark nodded *what?*

1.62a Eloise cursed Thalia.

  b Eloise cursed *whom?*

To perform this exercise correctly, one must have already located the direct object and classified it as human or nonhuman. We did not say, "Mark nodded *whom?*" or "Eloise cursed *what?*"

Through examples and a few observations, most people find that objects are as easy to recognize as subjects and verbs. To illustrate the value of the use of examples, you should try to find the direct objects in these sentences:

1.63   Henry swatted the fly.

1.64   The cook murdered his assistant.

1.65   Your son neglected his homework.

1.66   Ann waved her arm.

The objects are, of course, *the fly*, *his assistant*, *his homework*, and *her arm*.

Normally the subject precedes the verb and the direct object follows it, as in the following sentences:

1.67   The salesman shoved the customer.

1.68   The customer shoved the salesman.

We instantly recognize a difference in meaning if we interchange positions. This word order of **Subject–Verb–Object** is the most frequent in English. It is often abbreviated **SVO**.

Whenever we read or hear sentences in which this basic order is not maintained, we try to impose such an arrangement because word order is the only means we have in Modern English for indicating whether a noun is subject or object. We can illustrate our mental rearrangement of sentences by the following groups of words that do not conform to the basic pattern:

1.69   caught the man the ball

1.70   kicked the rock my cousin

1.71   the hole he dug

1.72   Perry a song sang

Most people do not just read these as lists of unpatterned words, but rather try to obtain meaningful structures. In each case the verb demands an animate subject, and only one of the nouns meets this criterion. Therefore, we are able to determine a probable subject and object for each sentence. If **1.70** had been *kicked my friend my cousin*, we would not know which of the following choices to make:

1.73   My friend kicked my cousin.

1.74   My cousin kicked my friend.

Note that in trying to arrive at a meaning for sentences **1.69–1.72**, we did not merely label one noun as subject and the other as object. We mentally rearranged them so that the subject came before the verb and the object came after it.

Even when we have other signals such as pronoun forms, we want to have the SVO order:

> **1.75** He understood her.
>
> **1.76** She understood him.
>
> **1.77** *He her understood.
>
> **1.78** *Understood him she.

He and *she* are subject forms, *him* and *her* object forms, as we can see from the preceding examples. Although these forms unambiguously mark the probable functions of the pronouns in **1.77–1.78**, we want the words arranged in the order of **1.75** or **1.76**.

Verbs that take direct objects are known as **transitive verbs**. Those that do not take objects are called **intransitive verbs**. Thus, the verbs in the following two sentences are transitive:

> **1.79** The baby *pinched* my nose.
>
> **1.80** I *cracked* the walnuts.

These are intransitive:

> **1.81** The vase *fell*.
>
> **1.82** The speaker *frowned*.

Once we recognize whether a verb takes an object or not, we know whether it is transitive or intransitive.

Some verbs permit deletion of their objects:

> **1.83a** Kathy sings *songs* well.
>
> **b** Kathy sings well.
>
> **1.84a** I answered the *question* correctly.
>
> **b** I answered correctly.
>
> **1.85a** She dressed *herself* quickly.
>
> **b** She dressed quickly.

Some grammarians have classified the verbs in the **b** sentences as intransitive. Others have argued that these verbs should be classified as transitive because they have the same meaning as the verbs in the **a** sentences and because direct objects can be readily supplied. The term **pseudo-intransitive** has been suggested for verbs with understood objects.

Another group of intransitive verbs may become transitive if they take an object that is related in form:

1.86a   They fought hard. (intransitive)
  b   They fought a good fight. (transitive)
1.87a   She sighed. (intransitive)
  b   She sighed a sigh of desperation. (transitive)

This object is known as a **cognate object**. It is usually modified by an adjective or a prepositional phrase.

When recognizing subjects, you learned not to mistake the object of a preposition for the subject:

1.88a   Several *bottles* were broken.
  b   *Several* of the bottles were broken.

The same caution is necessary when you find direct objects:

1.89a   I broke several *bottles*.
  b   I broke *several* of the bottles.
1.90a   We believed neither *answer*.
  b   We believed *neither* of the answers.

As with subjects, if you mark off the prepositional phrases, you will not be confused about what is the direct object.

In discussing subjects, we noticed three features: They normally precede verbs; verbs agree with them; and there are restrictions on the kinds of nouns that may function as subjects of certain verbs. There are similar features for objects. First of all, as we have seen, they normally follow the verb:

1.91   The electrician shocked *the onlookers*.

Second, object pronouns are in the objective form:

1.92a   She hated *him*.
  b   *She hated *he*.

Third, there are restrictions on the kinds of nouns that can function as objects of certain verbs:

> **1.93**   Robert burned *the letters*.
>
> **1.94**   *Robert burned *my industriousness*.

The object of *burn* has to be a solid, combustible substance.

ADVERBS AND ADVERBIAL NOUNS

In addition to subjects, verbs, and direct objects, many sentences contain adverbs. Although adverbs may appear in various places in a sentence, their most usual position is at the end. If the verb is transitive, they normally follow the direct object.

> **1.95a**   Betty opened the door.
> **b**   Betty opened the door *quickly*. (manner)
> **1.96a**   We saw her.
> **b**   We saw her *there*. (place)
> **1.97a**   Fred earned the money.
> **b**   Fred earned the money *yesterday*. (time)

An adverb following an intransitive verb should not be mistaken for a direct object:

> **1.98a**   The horse ran.
> **b**   The horse ran *fast*. (manner)
> **1.99a**   She slept.
> **b**   She slept *upstairs*. (place)
> **1.100a**   I yelled.
> **b**   I yelled *then*. (time)

In addition to adverbs, nouns may at times have an adverbial function:

> **1.101a**   He worked two *hours* at the office.

We know that *hours* is a noun because it takes a plural ending and is modified by the adjective *two*. You might be tempted to call *hours* a direct object until you notice that it can be questioned with "How long?" or replaced with *then*:

> **1.101b** *How long* did he work at the office?
>
> **c** He worked *then* at the office.

By contrast, we know that pronouns replace direct objects:

> **1.102a** He worked the *puzzle* at the office.
>
> **b** *What* did he work at the office?
>
> **c** He worked *it* at the office.

Neither *what* nor *it* can replace *two hours*. We call *hours* in **1.101a** an **adverbial noun**. We call it a noun rather than an adverb because it takes a plural ending and permits adjective modifiers. The term *adverbial noun* indicates that the word is a noun in form but that it functions as an adverb.

The best device for distinguishing between direct objects and adverbial nouns is substitution. If the structure can be replaced by a pronoun such as *what* or *it*, it is probably a direct object. We have to say *probably* because the structure could also be a subjective complement, as we shall see in the next chapter. On the other hand, if the structure can be replaced by an adverb such as *there, where, when, how much*, or *how long*, it is an adverb or an adverbial noun.

> **1.103a** We went *home*. (adverbial noun)
>
> **b** We went *there*. *We went *it*.
>
> **c** *Where* did we go? *What* did we go?
>
> **1.104a** Harry walked a *mile* this morning. (adverbial noun)
>
> **b** *How far* did Henry walk this morning?
>
> **1.105a** He slept all *day* and worked all *night*. (adverbial nouns)
>
> **b** *When* did he sleep? *When* did he work?
>
> **c** He slept *then*. He worked *then*.

Such verbs of quantity as *cost, weigh*, and *measure* take adverbial nouns when they are stative verbs. *Weigh* and *measure* take direct objects only when they are action verbs.

1.106a The postal employee weighed the *package*. (direct object)

    b *What* did the postal employee weigh?

    c The postal employee weighed *it*.

1.107a The package weighed six *pounds*. (adverbial noun)

    b *How much* did the package weigh?

Sometimes you will need to try several devices. For example, if you had tried questioning **1.107a** with *what*, you would have produced a satisfactory sentence:

1.107c *What* did the package weigh?

However, you can see from **1.107b** that *how much* is also possible, whereas only *what* is acceptable for **1.106a**. Also, you are not able to substitute *it* or *them* for *six pounds*.

PREPOSITIONS AND PARTICLES

Prepositional phrases may follow direct objects the same way adverbs do:

1.108 Susan opened the package *with care*. (manner)

1.109 I read the notice *under a street light*. (place)

1.110 Hank stopped the car *in the nick of time*. (time)

1.111 He closed his eyes *because of the sun*. (cause)

In addition, prepositional phrases may follow intransitive verbs:

1.112 She walked *with grace*. (manner)

1.113 We worked *beside a window*. (place)

1.114 The siren sounded *at noon*. (time)

1.115 We left *because of the heat*. (cause)

Be careful not to mistake the object of a preposition for a direct object.

Words that are used as prepositions in some sentences may be used differently in others:

1.116a Samantha looked up the chimney.

1.117a Samantha looked up the information.

Up the chimney qualifies as a prepositional phrase used adverbially because we may substitute adverbs for it:

1.116a Samantha looked *up the chimney*.
   b Samantha looked *there*.
   c *Where* did Samantha look?

We cannot make similar substitutions for sentence **1.117a**. In fact, *looked up* is a unit as opposed to *up the information*. We can make the following substitution:

1.117a Samantha *looked up* the information.
   b Samantha *sought* the information.

Notice that *up* in this sentence does not have the directional meaning that is the opposite of *down*. *Up* is neither a preposition nor an adverb here; rather, it is a **particle** attached to the verb. In some ways *look up*, meaning "seek," is like a compound. A combination like *look up* is known as a **verb-particle combination**. (This structure has been called by many additional names: *verb-adverb combination, group verb, phrasal verb, merged verb, poly-word verb*, to name a few.)

Only a few particles occur with any degree of frequency. *Up, down, out, in, off*, and *on* are the most common. Still fairly frequent are *about, across, around, over, through, to*, and *with*. All these words can also function as prepositions. The list of verbs, mostly of one syllable, that may have particles attached to them is much larger.

Some words almost never occur as verbs except in verb-particle combinations: *eke out, peter out, dole out, batten down, jack up, bone up*, and so on.

Several features of verb-particle combinations distinguish them from a succession of verb and adverb or of verb and preposition. First, the verb-particle combination has the meaning of a single verb. We can sometimes substitute a synonym:

1.118a They *put off* the meeting.
   b They *postponed* the meeting.
1.119a We *gave up*.
   b We *surrendered*.

Unfortunately, there is often no exact synonym because one reason for forming verb-particle combinations is that no verbs exist with the desired meanings. Nevertheless, the substitution of a verb with a *similar* meaning should usually be possible.

Second, the meaning of the combination may be different from that of the two words in isolation. In **1.118a** we are not actually *putting* anything, nor are we *giving* anything in **1.119a**. Yet there are other combinations in which both words retain their original meanings:

> **1.120a**   The outlaw *held up* his gun.
>
> **b**   The outlaw *raised* his gun.

In this sentence, he is literally holding the gun in an upward position. However, we can also use *hold up* in a sense in which neither *hold* nor *up* is thought of separately:

> **1.121a**   The outlaw *held up* the bank.
>
> **b**   The outlaw *robbed* the bank.

If he held anything, it was not a bank.

Third, a particle may be moved after a direct object:

> **1.122a**   The children *hung up* their clothes.
>
> **b**   The children *hung* their clothes *up*.

If the direct object is a pronoun, the particle must follow it:

> **1.122c**   *The children *hung up* them.
>
> **d**   The children *hung* them *up*.

We can contrast this structure with that of a verb followed by a prepositional phrase:

> **1.123a**   Jack ran up the hill.
>
> **b**   *Jack ran the hill up.
>
> **c**   Jack ran up it.
>
> **d**   *Jack ran it up. (where *it* means *hill*)

Because *up the hill* is a prepositional phrase, *up* may not be moved after its object, whether it is a noun or a pronoun.

1.124a   Jack ran up the bill.

b   Jack ran the bill up.

c   *Jack ran up it. (where *it* means *bill*)

d   Jack ran it up.

In this sentence *ran up* is a verb-particle combination. When the direct object is a noun, such as *bill*, the particle may follow either the verb or the object; however, when the object is a pronoun, the particle must follow the object, not the verb.

The feature of particle movement applies, of course, only to sentences containing direct objects. If the verb is intransitive, there is no possibility for moving the particle. Then you must rely on meaning and substitution:

1.125   We almost *passed out* because of the heat.

We recognize *passed out* as a verb-particle combination because it can be replaced with *fainted*.

Direct objects and object of prepositions are contrasted in the following sentences:

1.126a   We lived down that *incident*. (direct object)

b   We lived down that *lane*. (object of a preposition)

1.127a   I looked over my *paper* for errors. (direct object)

b   I looked over my *glasses* at her. (object of a preposition)

1.128a   Stephanie turned up her *nose* at us. (direct object)

b   Stephanie turned up that *street*. (object of a preposition)

You are able to move *down, over,* and *up* only when they are particles.

INDIRECT OBJECTS

We have seen that the usual place for adverbials is at the end:

1.129a   Edgar threw the ball *to Mike*.

We recognize *Edgar* as the subject, *threw* as the verb, *the ball* as the direct object, and *to Mike* as a prepositional phrase functioning as an adverbial of direction. If we moved the prepositional phrase before the direct object, the result would be awkward:

1.129b   Edgar threw *to Mike* the ball.

However, we can delete the preposition and produce an acceptable sentence:

1.129c   Edgar threw *Mike* the ball.

Mike now is known as an **indirect object**. The traditional definition of the indirect object as the one to whom or for whom the action is performed is usually fairly accurate.

Here are some more examples in which prepositional phrases are moved and converted into indirect objects:

1.130a   The Dean wrote a letter *to the student*.
   b   The Dean wrote *the student* a letter.
1.131a   The chef baked a birthday cake *for Ben*.
   b   The chef baked *Ben* a birthday cake.

The indirect object usually names a human or an animal, but a few verbs such as *give* may take inanimate indirect objects:

1.132   We gave *the wall* a fresh coat of paint.

We saw that direct objects occur with transitive verbs. Indirect objects occur with a small subclass of these verbs. Most common are certain verbs of motion: *throw, toss, send, pitch, give,* and the like. They also occur with such verbs as *bake, make, cook, build, pass,* and *bring*.

When a verb has both an indirect and a direct object, it is word order that signals the relationship: Subject–Verb–Indirect Object–Direct Object:

1.133   Your grandmother left you a message.

A sentence is seldom incomplete without an indirect object:

1.134a   Mr. Chapman wired me the money.
   b   Mr. Chapman wired the money.

1.135a   They gave us their old clothes.

b   They gave their old clothes.

1.136a   Janet's mother bought her a new dress.

b   Janet's mother bought a new dress.

However, without the indirect object, the sentences are less exact. If we try deleting the direct object, we run into problems:

1.134c   Mr. Chapman wired me.

1.135c   They gave us.

1.136c   Janet's mother bought her.

These sentences are not just less exact than the **a** versions; they have different meanings. The direct object is more basic than the indirect object.

A few verbs permit the deletion of the direct object:

1.137a   My attorney wrote me *a letter* about the matter.

b   My attorney wrote me about the matter.

In either version, consider *me* the indirect object.

When the direct object is a noun, the choice of expressing the beneficiary of the action as an indirect object or as the object of a preposition is usually only one of personal preference:

1.138a   Connie gave the present to her daughter.

b   Connie gave her daughter the present.

c   Connie gave the present to her.

d   Connie gave her the present.

This choice is not affected by whether the indirect object is a noun or a pronoun. When the direct object is a pronoun, however, there are restrictions:

1.138e   Connie gave it to her daughter.

f   *Connie gave her daughter it.

g   Connie gave it to her.

h   *Connie gave her it.

For most speakers of American English, only the prepositional-phrase structure is possible when the direct object is a pronoun.

British English accepts all the structures that are found in American English, but it also permits an additional one:

    1.138i   Connie gave it her.

The direct object precedes the indirect.

SUMMARY

We can summarize the main topics of this chapter by marking the basic elements in a few representative sentences. The abbreviations are obvious.

    1.139   The wind blew.
                 s   *v*

    1.140   Many people have left.
              s   *v*   *v*

    1.141   Many [of the people] have left.
            s   *v*   *v*

    1.142   [Behind the wall] was a garden.
                  v   *s*

    1.143   There is a fly [in my soup].
              v   *s*

    1.144   They will catch him soon.
           s   *v*   *v*   *do*

    1.145   She likes most people.
           s   *v*   *do*

    1.146   She likes most [of the people].
           s   *v*   *do*

    1.147   He walked a long way.
          s   *v*   *an*

    1.148   He looked up her address.
          s   *v*   *prt*   *do*

    1.149   The mouse ran [up the wall].
            s   *v*

    1.150   They gave me the message.
          s   *v*   *io*   *do*

EXERCISES

A. Enclose all prepositional phrases in parentheses and identify the major sentence elements:

s	subject	*do*	direct object
v	verb	*io*	indirect object
an	adverbial noun		

  1.   He studied six poems.
  2.   He studied six hours.

   3.   Most of the staff went home early.
   4.   She held up a sealed envelope.
   5.   Their eyes traveled up the wall.
   6.   The committee awarded her brother first prize.
   7.   She carried her work outside.
   8.   There should be a snack bar in this building.
   9.   I liked only part of the performance.
   10.   I fell an hour ago.
   11.   They made up their minds.
   12.   Next comes the main course of the meal.
   13.   She showed courage in her actions.
   14.   The judge granted us a recess.
   15.   They drifted several miles down the river.
   16.   Once upon a time there lived a princess in a far-off kingdom.
   17.   They must have told him.
   18.   Hal brought along a thick notebook.
   19.   All of the children ran for the clown.
   20.   The aides wrangled for an hour.

B. Illustrate each of the following patterns in an original sentence:

   1.   Subject–Intransitive Verb–Prepositional Phrase
   2.   Subject–Transitive Verb–Direct Object
   3.   Subject–Transitive Verb–Indirect Object–Direct Object
   4.   Subject–Intransitive Verb–Adverbial Noun
   5.   Subject–Transitive Verb–Particle–Direct Object

C. In each of the following sentences either the subject-verb or the verb-object combination is inappropriate. Explain why the combination is unsatisfactory and supply a more appropriate verb.

example: The strong winds hurt my house.
   Hurt is an inappropriate verb for *house* because it requires an animate object. *Damaged* would be a better choice.

   1.   The leaves cried.
   2.   I assassinated the weeds in the flower garden.

3. She winked her ears at me.
4. My bonds aged.
5. Did the aspirin heal your headache?
6. The manicurist sliced my fingernails.
7. The leopard giggled at its prey.
8. I embezzled a quarter from your purse.

chapter 2 ═══════════

Complements
and Appositives

In Chapter 1 we saw that transitive verbs are followed by direct objects and that some verbs permit both direct and indirect objects. In this chapter we will examine additional structures that follow the verb.

SUBJECTIVE COMPLEMENTS

You have already learned not to assume automatically that every noun following a verb is a direct object:

> **2.1** The dog chased the *porcupine*. (direct object)
> **2.2** The dog ran a long *way*. (adverbial noun)

There are other nouns placed after the verb that are neither objects nor adverbial nouns. Notice the different uses of *tax consultant* in the following sentences:

> **2.3** Mr. Roberts hit my *tax consultant*.
> **2.4** Mr. Roberts is my *tax consultant*.

In **2.3** *Mr. Roberts* and *tax consultant* name different people, but in **2.4** they name the same man. Also, in **2.3** we see that *tax consultant* is a direct object because it receives the action of the verb *hit*. We do not call *tax consultant* in **2.4** a direct object, but rather a **predicate noun**, a word that follows the verb and renames the subject. (Predicate nouns are also called **predicate nominatives**.)

Words that follow the verb and describe the subject are known as **predicate adjectives**:

> **2.5**   Your sister is *tall*.
>
> **2.6**   Grammar seems *easy*.

Predicate nouns and adjectives are often grouped together under the inclusive term **subjective complement**. A **complement** in grammar is a word or other structure that is needed to complete part of a sentence, usually a predicate. If you link the words *complement* and *complete*, you will never confuse *complement* and *compliment* ("praise") in spelling. A subjective complement is needed after the verb to complete the predicate and form a complete sentence.

> **2.7a**   *Cindy seems.
>
> **b**   Cindy seems *surprised*.

The word *subjective* is used because this complement renames or describes the subject.

A verb that takes a subjective complement is called a **linking verb** (or sometimes a **copulative verb**, or just a **copula**). As the term suggests, a linking verb *links* or *joins* a subject and a subjective complement. The most common linking verb, *be*, has little meaning in itself apart from equating elements:

> **2.8**   Springfield *is* the capital of Illinois.
>
> **2.9**   The leaves *were* yellow.

Other linking verbs have more meaning than *be*, but they all have a joining function.

Only a limited number of verbs are linking, and only a small subset of those permit predicate nouns. The most common are *be, become, remain, continue,* and *stay:*

> **2.10**   The cat became a nuisance.
> **2.11**   They remained friends.
> **2.12**   Thompson and Higgins continued partners.
> **2.13**   We stayed friends.

The verbs that take predicate nouns express states rather than actions. British English accepts a few additional verbs with predicate nouns:

> **2.14a**   I felt a fool.
> **2.15a**   She looked an intelligent person.

American English would normally have *like* after the verb:

> **2.14b**   I felt like a fool.
> **2.15b**   She looked like an intelligent person.

The most useful guide for distinguishing predicate nouns from direct objects is reference. If the subject and the word after the verb refer to different people or things, the latter is a direct object, provided that it meets all other tests (i.e., that it is not an adverbial noun or some other structure). On the other hand, if the two nouns or pronouns refer to the same person or thing, the one after the verb is a predicate noun.

Reflexive pronouns (those ending in *-self*) and reciprocals (*each other, one another*) are exceptional because they require other devices for classification. The reciprocals are always objects:

> **2.16a**   They hugged *each other*.

If you substitute another word for *each other*, you see that whatever follows *hugged* is a direct object:

> **2.16b**   They hugged *me*.

Similarly, you cannot use reference to determine how reflexive pronouns function, but you can substitute other nouns or pronouns for comparison:

> **2.17a**   Tom shot *himself*.
> **b**   Tom shot the *lieutenant*.

Lieutenant and *himself* both function as direct objects. A reflexive may also be an indirect object or the object of a preposition:

> **2.18a** I bought *myself* an electric toothbrush.
> **b** I bought an electric toothbrush for *myself*.

Occasionally a reflexive functions as a predicate noun:

> **2.19a** He is *himself* again.

If you substitute another word for *himself*, it is clearly a predicate noun:

> **2.19b** He is our *friend* again.

The meaning is changed slightly, but the structure remains the same. In summary, do not try classifying reflexive pronouns by reference; instead, substitute other nouns or pronouns for them and see how they function.

Before leaving predicate nouns, you should be cautioned against using *what* as the only device for recognizing direct objects:

> **2.20a** The coach is driving a *sports car*. (direct object)
> **b** *What* is the coach driving?
> **2.21a** The prize was a *sports car*. (predicate noun)
> **b** *What* was the prize?

Both predicate nouns and direct objects can be questioned with *what*. This question word is useful only in showing that the word it replaces is a noun.

Turning to predicate adjectives, we see that they may follow any of the verbs that take predicate nouns:

> **2.22** The trip *was* pleasant.
> **2.23** The room *became* stuffy.
> **2.24** They *remained* friendly.
> **2.25** The weather *continued* cold.
> **2.26** They *stayed* hostile.

There are additional linking verbs that take predicate adjectives but not predicate nouns:

2.27a   The receptionist *seemed* unhappy.
2.28a   They *appeared* nervous.
2.29a   His explanations *rang* false.
2.30a   The water *turned* green.

There are a few dozen more. If you cannot decide how a word after the verb functions, replace the verb with a form of *be:*

2.27b   The receptionist *was* unhappy.
2.28b   They *were* nervous.
2.29b   His explanations *were* false.
2.30b   The water *was* green.

The meaning is changed slightly, but the structure remains the same.

Verbs of the senses are often followed by predicate adjectives:

2.31   Your house smells odd.
2.32   The bread felt warm.
2.33   The soup tastes salty.
2.34   The flowers look lovely.
2.35   The music sounds heavenly.

These are linking verbs only when they name states. When they express actions, they are followed by direct objects or adverbs. Contrast sentence **2.31**, in which *smell* names a state, with the following:

2.36   The child smells the candy.
2.37   I smelled everywhere for the gas.

In **2.36**, *smell* is a transitive verb taking the direct object *candy*. In **2.37**, it is intransitive, with *everywhere* functioning as an adverb of place. When *smell* means "to sniff," it expresses an action.

When you are trying to distinguish between an adverb of manner and a predicate adjective, do not use the interrogative *how* or the suffix *-ly:*

2.38a   Her friend ran *awkwardly*. (adverb)

   b   *How* did her friend run?

2.39a   Her friend seemed *neighborly*. (predicate adjective)

   b   *How* did her friend seem?

Both structures may be questioned with *how*, and both may end in *-ly*. Adverbs of manner modify verbs, not nouns. *Awkwardly* in **2.38a** describes the manner of running. Predicate adjectives modify subjects, as *neighborly* does in **2.39a**. If you are having trouble deciding what a word modifies, as in **2.39a**, use one of these devices:

1. Substitute a form of *be* for the verb, as we did in **2.27–2.30**.

2. Substitute a few words that are clearly adjectives and some that are definitely adverbs for the word in question. Such adjectives as *awkward, graceful*, and *courageous* are possible in **2.39a**, but adverbs like *awkwardly, gracefully*, and *courageously* do not fit.

3. Place the word in question between an article or possessive and the subject noun. If it is an adjective, it can go in this position and modify the subject: *her awkward friend, her neighborly friend*. But if it is an adverb, it cannot fill this position: **her awkwardly friend, *her gracefully friend*.

Prepositional phrases may function as predicate adjectives in the same way as single-word adjectives do. They should be distinguished from adverbial prepositional phrases.

2.40a   My grandfather is *healthy*. (predicate adjective)

   b   My grandfather is *in good health*. (predicate adjective)

   c   My grandfather is *in the room*. (adverbial)

2.41a   I looked *foolish*. (predicate adjective)

   b   I looked *like a fool*. (predicate adjective)

   c   I ran *like a fool*. (adverbial)

If a prepositional phrase functions as a predicate adjective, you should be able to substitute a single-word adjective with a similar meaning.

APPOSITIVES

An **appositive** follows a noun and renames it:

> **2.42** Evelyn, my *niece*, wrote the letter.
> **2.43** This is a picture of my first car, a 1954 *Chevrolet*.
> **2.44** I am taking a course in semantics, the *study* of meaning.

Although most appositives are nouns, some are phrases or clauses, as you will see in later chapters.

Appositives can be paraphrased as predicate nouns:

> **2.45a** I was talking to Ben, Anne's *husband*. (appositive)
> **b** Ben is Anne's *husband*. (predicate noun)

Even though appositives and predicate nouns rename other nouns, there are important differences between them. The predicate noun is separated from the noun it renames by a linking verb, but the appositive follows immediately:

> **2.46** Mr. Richardson became *my worst enemy*. (predicate noun)
> **2.47** Mr. Richardson, *my worst enemy*, snubbed me. (appositive)

Another difference is that the predicate noun always renames the subject, whereas the appositive can rename any noun in the sentence:

> **2.48** Mr. Smith, *my teacher*, left this. (renames the subject)
> **2.49** He hit Earl, *Charlie's brother*. (renames the direct object)
> **2.50** That woman is my neighbor, *Mrs. Reese*. (renames the predicate noun)
> **2.51** He was talking to the coach, *an old bore*. (renames the object of a preposition)

Although the appositive and the predicate noun provide similar information, we make a distinction between them.

OBJECTIVE COMPLEMENTS

An **objective complement** is a word that completes the predicate and describes or renames a direct object or the object of a preposition:

2.52   We consider him a *fool*.

2.53   We consider him *foolish*.

As these examples show, an objective complement may be a noun or an adjective. There are no terms for distinguishing between the two, as predicate noun and predicate adjective subdivide subjective complements. Rather, we refer to both adjectives and nouns as just objective complements. Here are a few more examples:

2.54   They named the baby *Carolyn*.

2.55   She dyed her hair *green*.

2.56   We painted the town *red*.

Objective complements may follow objects of prepositions:

2.57   I always sleep with one eye *open*.

2.58   Don't talk with your mouth *full*.

Also, prepositional phrases may function as objective complements, just as they do as subjective complements:

2.59a   We kept our instruments *orderly*.

   b   We kept our instruments *in order*.

2.60a   We consider them *friends*.

   b   We consider them *as friends*.

2.61a   The nurse found the baby *healthy*.

   b   The nurse found the baby *in good health*.

You saw that the term *subjective complement* is used because the word renames or describes a subject and is needed to complete the predicate. The term *objective complement* is similar. In addition to renaming or describing a direct object or the object of a preposition, it is usually needed to complete the meaning of the verb. Notice the differences in meaning in the following pairs of sentences:

2.62a Someone left the door ajar.

  b Someone left the door.

2.63a The decorator made the room cheerful.

  b The decorator made the room.

2.64a Everyone considers you a good choice.

  b Everyone considers you.

The verbs have different meanings in the two versions.

There are other verbs, however, in which omission of the objective complement is possible:

2.65a The members elected Allan president.

  b The members elected Allan.

2.66a We painted the box yellow.

  b We painted the box.

The meaning of the verb is not changed, but the sentence is less exact.

You may find yourself pausing at times over structures that may be either objective complements or appositives.

2.67 She called her son Carl. (objective complement)

2.68 She called her son, Carl. (appositive)

An appositive is never needed to complete the predicate, but an objective complement usually is. (There are exceptions, as we saw in **2.65** and **2.66**.) We can leave out *Carl* in **2.68** without altering the meaning of the verb, but we cannot do so in **2.67**. Also, if we interchange *her son* and *Carl*, we change the meaning radically in **2.67**, but make only small changes with the appositive in **2.68**. The sentence with the appositive could be recast as two sentences:

2.69 She called her son. His name was Carl.

No such paraphrase is possible with the objective complement.

Another structure that might seem like an objective complement is the verb-particle combination:

2.70a I made the bed neat. (objective complement)

2.71a I made the bed up. (verb-particle)

When the direct object is a noun, a particle may go after the verb or after the object; the objective complement does not have this flexibility:

2.70b *I made neat the bed.
2.71b   I made up the bed.

Whereas both *up* and *neat* complete the meaning of the verb in a sense, we treat *made up* as though it were a word unit, whereas *made neat* is not thought of as a word. Dictionaries list *make up*, but they do not have an entry for *make neat*. In addition, *neat* clearly modifies the object *bed*, but *up* does not. Finally, particles are limited to a small number of words that can also be prepositions or adverbs; objective complements are nouns or adjectives. Here are two more sentences that illustrate the difference between particles and objective complements:

2.72   The speaker left a word *out*. (particle)
2.73   The speaker left the audience *alone* for a few minutes. (objective complement)

You should use the tests we just discussed for *make up* and *make neat*.

With the objective complement, we have completed our introduction to the most important uses of nouns and pronouns. We may summarize them by using examples:

2.74   The *cat* purred. (subject)
2.75   We wrote the *letter*. (direct object)
2.76   The leaf floated a long *way*. (adverbial noun)
2.77   She gave *Tim* a piece of cake. (indirect object)
2.78   The shoe is under the *bed*. (object of a preposition)
2.79   You are a real *jewel*. (predicate noun)
2.80   Your partner, a real *jewel*, is stupid. (appositive)
2.81   She called me a *liar*. (objective complement)

ADVERBIAL COMPLEMENTS

An intransitive verb does not need a complement after it:

2.82   We *sat*.
2.83   The sun *shone*.

Other verbs require something else in the predicate if the sentence is to be complete. This essential element is an object or a complement. Some grammarians include objects under the category of complement.

> **2.84a** *Aunt Harriet sent.
> **b** Aunt Harriet sent the *money*. (direct object)
> **2.85a** *The town seemed.
> **b** The town seemed *deserted*. (subjective complement)
> **2.86a** *The new facts render your argument.
> **b** The new facts render your argument *void*. (objective complement)

At times, the omission of the objective complement does not make a sentence incomplete, but it changes the meaning of the verb:

> **2.87a** Your questions are driving me.
> **b** Your questions are driving me *crazy*.

For the intended meaning of *drive*, the objective complement is necessary.

In addition to the complements that we have discussed, there are **adverbial complements** (adverbs or prepositional phrases) that are necessary for completing certain verbs. You remember that most adverbial modifiers are optional:

> **2.88a** Sarah opened the door.
> **b** Sarah opened the door *immediately*.
> **2.89a** It was raining.
> **b** It was raining *in sheets*.

The adverbial provides desired information, but its omission does not make the sentence incomplete.

Now look at the following verbs, both with and without an adverbial:

> **2.90a** *The scoundrel lurked.
> **b** The scoundrel lurked *outside*.
> **c** The scoundrel lurked *in the corridor*.
> **2.91a** *The pencil was.

    b The pencil was *there*.

    c The pencil was *under the desk*.

2.92a *I glanced.

    b I glanced *inside*.

    c I glanced *at the page*.

We call the required adverb or prepositional phrase an adverbial complement, as opposed to the optional adverbials in sentences such as **2.88** and **2.89**.

    Some verbs require adverbial complements beginning with specific prepositions:

2.93a *We have disposed.

    b We have disposed *of our old clothes*.

2.94a *They depend.

    b They depend *on each other*.

To illustrate the adverbial complement, see how much freedom you have in completing the following sentences. If they will not stand alone as they are, how many different prepositions can you use to begin the required phrase?

    2.95   He came to grips.

    2.96   We brooded.

    2.97   They got rid.

    2.98   The words hung.

    2.99   You should apply yourself.

    2.100 She sank her teeth.

    2.101 Could you talk him?

You may accept two of these as they stand, but for each verb there is only one preposition that is usual.

    Since the preposition introducing an adverbial complement may look like a particle, let us compare them:

    2.102a She looked *up* the information.

    2.103a She looked *after* my needs.

A particle may come before or after a noun direct object, but a preposition must precede its object:

> **2.102b** She looked the information *up*.
> **2.103b** *She looked my needs *after*.

If the direct object is a pronoun, the particle must follow it:

> **2.102c** She looked it *up*.
> **d** *She looked *up* it.
> **2.103c** *She looked them *after*.
> **d** She looked *after* them.

Both particles and complements are essential to the verb, but you can easily distinguish them if you use a few tests such as these.

QUESTIONS

In Chapter 1, you learned that inverted word order could make it difficult for you to recognize subjects. You were advised to recast sentences in normal order before you analyzed them:

> **2.104a** There is a fly in the room.
> **b** A fly is in the room.
> **2.105a** Behind the chair was a bloody knife.
> **b** A bloody knife was behind the chair.

Once you have the sentence in normal word order, you have no difficulty telling how the various elements function.

In addition to expletives and introductory adverbials, questions invert the word order of a sentence. Whenever you need to analyze the parts of a question, convert it into a declarative statement:

> **2.106a** Are you our new secretary?
> **b** You are our new secretary.
> **2.107a** Whom are they watching?
> **b** They are watching whom.

Although texts in linguistics usually study the formation of questions in detail, for the kind of sentence analysis you will be performing in this book, it is enough to be able to convert questions into statements. The easiest way to make this conversion is to answer the question with a complete sentence:

2.108a   Is Mike going with us?
   b   Mike is going with us.
2.109a   Who opened the door?
   b   I opened the door.
2.110a   Where are you going?
   b   I am going there.

Notice that in the answer you will be replacing the question words (*who, which, what, where, when, why, how*) with specific nouns, pronouns, or adverbs; however, this substitution does not affect the structure of the sentence.

Telling how a word functions in a question is not difficult if you recast the sentence as a statement:

2.111a   *What* did she become?
   b   She became a *lawyer*. (subjective complement)
2.112a   *What* did they name the baby?
   b   They named the baby *Kevin*. (objective complement)
2.113a   *Whom* are you imitating?
   b   I am imitating *you*. (direct object)

Remember to recast questions as statements by answering them in complete sentences.

EXERCISES

A.   Tell how the nouns and pronouns function:

   1.   She owns a Ford.
   2.   My new car is a Ford.
   3.   The members have elected me president of the club.
   4.   Has Sandra gulped down the tea?
   5.   What did Fred send Pat?
   6.   I weighed the turtle.
   7.   The turtle weighed thirty pounds.

8. She made him a good citizen.
9. She made him a good sandwich.
10. I taught myself to swim.
11. The Nelsons spent six years in Canada.
12. In spite of your actions, we consider you our friend.
13. He should have remained president.
14. Someone sewed up my pocket.
15. How much do kind words cost?
16. I blew out the smoke.
17. Were you talking to your friend George?
18. The ground bore traces of a catastrophe.
19. From the village came a small boy.
20. We will order you a hamburger.

B. Tell how the italicized words function:

1. The room got *hot* suddenly.
2. The firemen went *home* later.
3. I wrung out my *shirt*.
4. You should sweep the room *clean*.
5. Harold Martin, my *nephew*, wrote the article.
6. I turned *forty* last month.
7. They turned the *corner* suddenly.
8. She showed off her new *shoes*.
9. Don't cry *yourself sick*.
10. He arose a new *man* the next *morning*.
11. Don't mix up your *words*.
12. Have you written your *father*?
13. *What* did you send your *brother George*?
14. He made *himself* a new *toy*.
15. He hasn't been *himself* lately.
16. We went several *miles*.
17. The milk went *sour*.
18. I dug out my old *sweater*.
19. I ran out the *door*.
20. The neighbors looked *friendly*.

C. Write original sentences using the verbs as indicated:

1. *appear*, linking
2. *appear*, intransitive
3. *feel*, transitive
4. *feel*, linking
5. *grow*, intransitive
6. *grow*, linking
7. *grow*, transitive
8. *work*, transitive
9. *work*, intransitive
10. *taste*, transitive
11. *taste*, linking
12. *remain*, intransitive
13. *remain*, linking
14. *shake*, transitive
15. *shake*, intransitive
16. *shake*, linking

D. Each of the following sentences contains a word ending in the letters *-ly*. Classify each as an adjective, an adverb, or a noun, and justify your answers.

1. He choked the cat cruelly.
2. Hank was really sorry.
3. Your cake tasted ghastly.
4. He is our ally.
5. The champagne was bubbly.
6. She felt lonely.
7. Lois dropped the hint delicately.
8. He is a bully.
9. They drink wine occasionally.
10. Your suggestion sounds beastly.

chapter 3 ═══════════

The Verb Phrase

A sentence contains various kinds of information, such as the meanings of the individual words and any undertones they may convey:

> **3.1** The fireman was ostensibly looking for the hose.

We understand the main words *fireman, ostensibly, looking,* and *hose*. In addition, we realize from the use of *ostensibly* that he was probably looking for something else while pretending to hunt for the hose. With our choice of words we also indicate the level of formality we wish to convey, as seen in the following sentences:

> **3.2** We could see a sandwich on the plate.
> **3.3** The kids are getting sort of wild.
> **3.4** One's selection of vocabulary affects the style of the composition.

Sentence **3.2** would be appropriate almost anywhere, but **3.3** belongs exclusively to informal conversations, and **3.4** would be more likely to appear in writing than in conversation.

In addition to the meanings of individual words and their levels of appropriateness, a sentence contains other information, such as that expressed by the relationship between subject and verb, that between the verb and its complements, or that provided by adverbials. We have seen this information illustrated in the last two chapters.

We may also want to indicate the time of an action or state, its nature (in progress, completed, recurrent), or the speaker's attitude toward it (a promise, obligation, prediction, and so on). This kind of information is expressed in part by adverbials but also by the form of the verb.

PAST TENSE

Certain adverbials of time clearly refer to past actions or states: *yesterday, last week, the year before last, in 1960*. Others may refer to the past, depending upon the time of utterance: *in January, Monday, this afternoon*. The past-tense form of the verb must accompany these adverbials. In the following pairs of sentences, the second is marked with an asterisk to indicate that it is not possible:

> **3.5a** We moved to our new house last week.
>
> **b** *We move to our new house last week.
>
> **3.6a** Yesterday he opened a bank account.
>
> **b** *Yesterday he opens a bank account.

We refer to the form of the verb as its **tense** and the meaning expressed as the **time** of the action or state.

Most verbs in English form the past tense in writing by adding the ending -*ed* to infinitives. In Chapter 7, we shall have more to say about the infinitive, but for now it will suffice to say that this is the form under which verbs are entered in a dictionary. That is, we find such entries as *eat, sleep*, and *open*—the infinitive forms— not *eats, ate, eaten, sleeps, slept, opened*, or *opens*. We can illustrate past-tense formation with a few examples:

Infinitive	Past Tense
look	looked
clasp	clasped
dial	dialed
pour	poured
seem	seemed
delay	delayed
sew	sewed
head	headed

With some words various spelling conventions cause additional changes: doubling a final consonant (*slap, slapped*), dropping the final *e* (*hope, hoped*), changing a final *y* to *i* (*carry, carried*), and the like. These changes result from conventions that are more general than just past-tense formation. All that is really relevant to the past tense is the ending *-ed*.

Some verbs form the past tense with *-t* rather than *-ed* and often with a change of the vowel as well:

Infinitive	Past Tense
buy	bought
leave	left
send	sent
bend	bent
feel	felt
mean	meant

A few verbs have two past-tense forms—one in *-ed* and one in *-t:*

Infinitive	Past Tense
spill	spilled, spilt
burn	burned, burnt
spoil	spoiled, spoilt

Verbs whose past tenses end in *-t* are not many, but they may occur frequently.

Elementary grammars of Modern English usually refer to verbs with the ending *-ed* as **regular verbs** and all others as **irregular verbs**. This classification is based upon two facts: (1) most verbs today form their past tenses with *-ed*, and (2) new verbs entering the language are formed after this pattern (e.g., *escalated, bulldozed*). Although other classifications are desirable for talking about earlier stages of the language, this one is unobjectionable for statements about Modern English.

Examples of irregular verbs can be seen below:

Infinitive	Past Tense
sing	sang
go	went
do	did
be	was, were
ride	rode

When we speak of an action in the past, we may indicate that it occurred on one or more specific occasions or that it occurred habitually:

3.7 The cat *scratched* me when I tried to pick it up.

3.8 Yesterday the cat *scratched* me twice.

3.9 The cat *scratched* me every time I tried to pick it up.

Sentences **3.7** and **3.8** illustrate specific acts, **3.9** habitual action. Often verbs denoting habitual acts can be paraphrased with *would:*

3.10 The cat *would scratch* me every time I tried to pick it up.

Such a paraphrase is not possible for specific actions. Adverbials of frequency such as *usually, normally, every day, always,* and the like may occur with verbs denoting habitual action.

There are three chief uses of the past tense in English:

1. To express actions and states in past time.

3.11 Maureen *drove* to work this morning.

3.12 The elephant *drank* the water.

3.13 Everyone *remained* calm.

3.14 The flight attendant *seemed* unhappy.

2. To express past truths that are no longer valid and habitual actions that no longer occur.

3.15 At one time, the Mediterranean *was* the center of the civilized world.

3.16 I always *went* to bed before midnight in those days.

3. To preserve tense sequence even though the state that is named is still in effect.

3.17a He believes everyone *is* corrupt.

    b He believed everyone *was* corrupt.

3.18a She says she *knows* the combination.

    b She said she *knew* the combination.

3.19a I said, "The train *is* late."

  b I said that the train *was* late.

Some people prefer the present in **3.18b** and **3.19b** if the state is still in existence:

3.18c She said she *knows* the combination.

3.19c I said that the train *is* late.

Both **b** and **c** versions are found in edited writing.

PRESENT TENSE

In contrast to the past tense is the present, which is formed either with the unchanged infinitive or with the addition of *-s*. This latter form is found only with verbs whose subjects are singular nouns or pronouns such as *he, she,* or *it*. We can refer to these pronouns and nouns collectively as **third person** (i.e., the one spoken about rather than the speaker or the one spoken to). We may illustrate the third-person singular ending in a sample conjugation of the present tense:

I read	we read
you read	you read
he reads	they read

For nouns we can illustrate with *that girl* (singular) and *those girls* (plural):

that girl reads	those girls read

Since nouns that are subjects are always third person, all we have to be concerned with is whether they are singular or plural.

Because we commonly divide time into past, present, and future, it would be natural to assume that the tenses of the verb correspond to these times. We can, in fact, provide sentences in which such a correspondence exists:

3.20 I saw the snake last week. (past time, past tense)

3.21 I see the snake now. (present time, present tense)

3.22 I shall see the snake later. (future time, future tense)

The adverbs reinforce the time of the state.

However, when we change to action verbs we encounter problems with the use of the simple present tense for present time:

> **3.23** I break the window now.
> **3.24** I eat the cake now.
> **3.25** I catch the cat now.

These are odd, but they would be possible if we were demonstrating some process such as cooking:

> **3.26** Now I add two eggs.

We have not, therefore, marked them with asterisks.

The uses for the present tense are more numerous than those for the past, but you can learn them easily if you distinguish between action verbs and those that name states.

1. Use the present tense to express habitual actions.

> **3.27** I *skip* lunch on Mondays.
> **3.28** Whenever the elevator *stops*, she *gets* off.

Except for a few sentences beginning with *there* and *here* ("Here *comes* your daughter" or "There *goes* your bus"), present actions are expressed by the present progressive tense, not by the simple present. The progressive tenses are discussed later in this chapter.

2. Use the present tense to express a present state.

> **3.29** You *look* better now.
> **3.30** At this moment they *are* in Alaska.

3. Use the present tense for general truths.

> **3.31** Gold *costs* more than silver.
> **3.32** December *is* a summer month in Australia.

4. Use the present tense as an historical present to relate most actions and states in literature.

3.33 When Nicholas *feels* the hot poker, he *yells*, "Water!"

3.34 Lear *becomes* so upset with Kent he *banishes* him.

The historical present is also used for stage directions in plays:

3.35 Brian *glances* at the clock.

5. Use the present tense in independent clauses to express future time if you are confident the action will occur.

3.36 We *begin* our vacation tomorrow.

3.37 She *leaves* for Seattle next week.

The future tense is also possible in these sentences. If the action is one of which you are not confident, you must use the future tense:

3.38 It *will rain* tomorrow. (Not "It *rains* tomorrow.")

6. Use the present tense in most adverb clauses and in some noun clauses to express future time. Future tense is usually not permitted in these kinds of dependent clauses.

3.39 When you *see* her, she will be wearing her new coat.

3.40 I hope you *have* a good time at the convention.

3.41 They will not believe you unless you *produce* the evidence.

3.42 If he *lives* through this ordeal, he will owe his life to you.

FUTURE TENSE

There is, strictly speaking, no future form of the verb in English in the way that there is in some other languages such as Latin, where we find forms like these:

vocō	I am calling
vocābam	I was calling
vocābō	I shall call

English has distinct forms for present and past (*calls, called*), but it has to add words to indicate futurity. In earlier times English grammarians tried to find equivalents for the Latin verb forms, and they said that the future tense in English is formed by adding *shall* or *will* to the infinitive: *shall call, will call.*

However, futurity in English is more often expressed by means other than by *will* and *shall*. In each of the following sentences future time is clearly meant, yet only the first of them uses *will:*

3.43   The sale will end tomorrow.

3.44   The sale ends tomorrow.

3.45   The sale is going to end tomorrow.

3.46   The sale should end tomorrow.

3.47   The sale could end tomorrow.

3.48   The sale must end tomorrow.

We could easily find even other means of expressing future time. The adverb *tomorrow* can function with several helping verbs to mark futurity; in fact, it can even be used with the present-tense form, as **3.44** shows.

In spite of all the ways we can express future time in English, only those with *will* and *shall* are called future tense. For those people who use both *shall* and *will* rather than *will* exclusively, here are the rules. Use *shall* in the first person and *will* in the second and third persons to express a simple prediction about the future. (The only subjects that are first person are *I* and *we;* all others are second or third person.)

3.49a   I shall probably receive a card from him.

   b   They will probably receive a card from him.

Reverse the choice to express a promise, a demand, or a threat:

3.50a   I will repay the money.

   b   Henry shall repay the money.

Notice the contrast between the following prediction and threat:

3.51a   We shall be late. (prediction)

   b   We will not tolerate your lies. (threat)

In questions, the use of *will* in first person, as well as in second and third persons, suggests a prediction, whereas *shall* indicates volition:

> **3.52a** Where will we sit? (prediction)
> **b** Where shall we sit? (volition)

Whereas *shall* is still widely used in many parts of the English-speaking world, it has become rare in American English except for questions.

PROGRESSIVE TENSES

Unless they name habitual actions or general truths, verbs of action normally refer to completed acts:

> **3.53** Sally cursed me.
> **3.54** The postman rang the doorbell.
> **3.55** We wrote the letter.

We may also comment on actions that are in progress:

> **Present Progressive:** I am reading.
> **Past Progressive:** I was reading.
> **Future Progressive:** I shall be reading.

The main verb in a progressive tense is in the **present participial** form. All present participles in English end in the suffix *-ing*. (This is one of the few exceptionless rules in English grammar.) The present participle is accompanied by a form of the auxiliary verb *be*, and it is the form of *be* that determines whether the verb phrase is present, past, or future progressive. The present progressive has the forms *am, is,* or *are,* according to the subject. The past progressive takes *was* or *were,* depending upon whether the subject is singular or plural. And the future progressive is formed with *shall be* or *will be* plus the present participle. Notice that the main verb remains unchanged for the three progressive tenses.

The progressive tenses are used for commenting on actions in progress without regard to their beginning or end. The **past progressive** expresses an action that was ongoing at the same time as another past action:

3.56 I *was singing* when he entered the room.

3.57 As they *were opening* the door, they heard a strange sound.

In **3.56**, the act of singing was in progress when another past action took place: his entering the room. In **3.57**, opening the door was occurring at the time the sound was heard. Occasionally the past progressive is used with an adverbial of time instead of a second verb:

3.58 She *was working* at Hudson's then.

Such structures are more usual with habitual actions than with others.

The **present progressive** is used to express an action that is occurring at the present time, one that is habitual, or one that will take place in the future:

3.59 I *am watching* you. (occurring now)

3.60 She *is opening* the window. (occurring now)

3.61 They *are* always *reading* my mail. (habitual)

3.62 We *are working* late every night this week. (habitual)

3.63 He *is leaving* for Spain next week. (future)

3.64 You can tell me while we *are eating*. (future meaning in a dependent clause)

The **future progressive tense** is used to express an action that will be in progress at the same time as another future action:

3.65 They *will be rehearsing* when we get there.

3.66 When you see her, she *will be packing*.

This tense is like the past progressive in that one verb is usually linked to another. The other verb does not have to be in the future tense; it merely has to express future time.

PERFECT TENSES

In addition to the progressive tenses, there are perfect tenses, as illustrated here:

Present Perfect: Greg has written.

Past Perfect: Greg had written.

Future Perfect: Greg will have written.

The present perfect is always formed with *has* or *have*, the past perfect is formed with *had*, and the future perfect is formed with *will have* or *shall have*. Since both the present perfect and the past perfect take place in past time, be sure to distinguish them by the form of the auxiliary *have*.

The form of the main verb in the perfect tenses is called the **past participle**. For most verbs the past participle has the same form as the past tense:

Infinitive	Past Tense	Past Participle
drop	dropped	(have) dropped
jump	jumped	(have) jumped
comb	combed	(have) combed

Other verbs, however, have distinct forms in the past tense and the past participle:

Infinitive	Past Tense	Past Participle
drive	drove	(have) driven
choose	chose	(have) chosen
begin	began	(have) begun
go	went	(have) gone
be	was	(have) been

Verbs that form their past participles with *-ed* are known as regular verbs; those that use other means of formation are called irregular. This classification is the same as that for past-tense forms.

The perfect tenses are used to express actions that occur before other actions or to express states that begin before other actions or states. The **past perfect tense** is used to express an action or state that existed before another past action or state:

3.67   I learned that he *had quit* his job.

3.68   He knew that his partner *had died*.

3.69   After he *had read* the letter, he burned it.

In each of these sentences the action named in the past perfect tense took place prior to that named by the other verb.

The **present perfect tense** expresses an action that occurred recently enough in the past to have an effect on the present:

3.70 Lucy *has mailed* your letter.

3.71 I *have finished* my correspondence.

This tense is also used to express a state that began in the past and is continuing into the present:

3.72 We *have lived* in Dallas for six years.

3.73 She *has been* chairman for two months.

Whereas the present perfect tense of an action verb must name an event in the recent past, the only requirement for stative verbs is that the state still be in existence:

3.74 Life *has existed* on earth for millions of years.

The **future perfect tense** expresses an action that will occur before another future action; it also expresses a state that will begin before another future action or state:

3.75 We *will have finished* by the time you arrive.

3.76 On September 23, he *will have been* our secretary longer than any of his predecessors.

In **3.75**, the act of finishing precedes the future act of arriving. As **3.76** shows, the act or state expressed by the future perfect tense may precede a date or time rather than an action.

PERFECT PROGRESSIVE TENSES

The perfect progressive tenses are formed by combining both auxiliaries *have* and *be* with the main verb:

Present Perfect Progressive: It has been snowing.

Past Perfect Progressive: It had been snowing.

Future Perfect Progressive: It will have been snowing.

It is the first auxiliary that tells whether the tense is present, past, or future perfect progressive. After the auxiliary *will* we find the infinitive form of the next verb, which is *have* in this tense. Similarly, after the auxiliary *have* the next verb is a past participle: *been*. Finally, after the progressive auxiliary *be*, we find the present participle *snowing*. Also notice that the order of the auxiliaries is modal (*will*), then *have*, then *be*. Other combinations, such as **has will be snowing*, are not possible.

The **past perfect progressive** expresses an action or state that began before another past action or state and was still in progress:

3.77 He *had been driving* for ten hours when he stopped.

Since the driving began before the stopping, the verb is in the past perfect. The driving was also in progress when he began to stop; hence, the progressive tense is also needed. It is the combination of progressive and prior action that warrants the perfect progressive tense. Here is another example with a stative verb:

3.78 They *had been living* in that house only two weeks when they learned it had termites.

The state of living in the house began before that of learning about the termites, and it was still in effect.

The **present perfect progressive tense** expresses an action or state that began in the past and is still continuing:

3.79 We *have been painting* for over an hour.
3.80 She *has been cheating* on her exam.

The **future perfect progressive tense** expresses an action or state that will begin before another future action or state and still be in progress:

3.81 I *shall have been studying* for over an hour when you call.
3.82 By the time they miss the money, the thief *will have been gambling* with it for nearly a week.

Although the future perfect progressive tense is found only rarely, it is needed at times.

The following synopsis reviews the forms of the various tenses:

Present	They sing.
Past	They sang.
Future	They will sing.
Present Progressive	They are singing.
Past Progressive	They were singing.
Future Progressive	They will be singing.
Present Perfect	They have sung.
Past Perfect	They had sung.
Future Perfect	They will have sung.
Present Perfect Progressive	They have been singing.
Past Perfect Progressive	They had been singing.
Future Perfect Progressive	They will have been singing.

MOOD

In addition to giving the time an action occurred, as we do with the tense of the verb, we make other statements about the action, such as whether it is a fact or a hypothetical act (such as a wish), whether it is a command or a statement, and the like. This information is given by the **mood** (or **mode**) of the verb. There are three moods: *indicative*, *imperative*, and *subjunctive*.

The **indicative mood** is used to state a fact or to ask a question:

3.83   The potato *originated* in the Americas.

3.84   He *sees* you.

3.85   *Are* you satisfied with our product?

Information stated as a fact need not be true:

3.86   I *am* a thousand years old.

3.87   Two plus two *equals* five.

The **imperative mood** is used as one means of expressing commands:

3.88   *Open* the door.

3.89   *Read* the directions before you assemble the cabinet.

3.90   *Give* me your money.

The form of the imperative verb is the same as that of the infinitive, not that of the present tense, as we can see with *be:*

    3.91 *Be* quiet.

The subject of an imperative verb is the understood pronoun *you*.

    The **subjunctive mood** is usually divided into a past subjunctive and a present subjunctive, according to the form of the verb. The **past subjunctive** has the same form as the past indicative: *knew, opened, jumped,* and the like. When the verb is *be*, the past subjunctive is always *were*, never *was*.

    3.92 I wish I *lived* in Italy.
    3.93 She wishes she *were* there now.

The past subjunctive is used to express a condition contrary to fact, such as a wish or other rearrangement of reality. In **3.92,** I am stating that I do not live in Italy, and in **3.93** she is not there. Notice that the past subjunctive relates a present or future act or state, even though it is like the past indicative in form.

    Modals follow the same principle as other verbs: The present form is used for the indicative only, but the past form may be either indicative or subjunctive:

Present Form	Past Form
can	could
may	might
will	would
shall	should

There is another modal, *must*, but it does not have a subjunctive. Similarly, such semi-modals as *ought to* and *used to* are exclusively indicative. The subjunctive with modals can be seen in the following sentences. In each example, both verbs are in the same mood:

    3.94a Now that he *is* rich, he *will buy* a new car. (indicative)
        b If he *were* rich, he *would buy* a new car. (subjunctive)
    3.95a You *can help* me if you *are* not busy. (indicative)
        b You *could help* me if you *were* not busy. (subjunctive)

3.96a If I *look* like you aaafffter the plastic surgery, I *will shoot* myself. (indicative)

b If I *looked* like you, I *would shoot* myself. (subjunctive)

Notice that statements of fact and most possibilities are expressed in the indicative mood; the subjunctive is used for those that the speaker or writer considers contrary to fact.

A special form of the past subjunctive is the perfect form, used for conditions contrary to fact in the past:

3.97 If she *had been* there, we *would have seen* her.

3.98 I wish I *had known* his address.

The following sentence contrasts present and past time with the subjunctive:

3.99a If he *were* more polite, he *would make* fewer enemies.

b If he *had been* more polite, he *would have made* fewer enemies.

The **a** version indicates present or future time; the **b** version indicates the past.

Although *would have* in conditional clauses beginning with *if* is in spoken use in many parts of the United States, it is considered nonstandard in writing:

3.100a If he *would have been* more polite, he would have made fewer enemies. (nonstandard for written English)

b If he *had been* more polite, he would have made fewer enemies. (standard English)

3.101a If the cards *would have gone* to someone else, we would have been embarrassed. (nonstandard for writing)

b If the cards *had gone* to someone else, we would have been embarrassed. (standard)

Notice that the structure with *would have* is acceptable in independent clauses, such as *would have made* and *would have been* in the above examples.

The **present subjunctive** is formed from the infinitive form of the verb without *to*. It is most distinctive in the form *be* and the third-person singular forms of other verbs, which lack the *-s* ending:

    3.102 We recommend that you *be* on time.

    3.103 It is important that she *stay* for an extra hour.

The present subjunctive has two uses. The first is in noun clauses beginning with *that* when they follow certain verbs (*recommend, suggest, demand, insist*, etc.), nouns (*recommendation, insistence*, etc.), and adjectives (*necessary, essential*, etc.). In meaning, this use of the present subjunctive is closer to the imperative than to other subjunctives because it expresses a semi-command.

    The second use of the present subjunctive exists in certain set phrases like the following:

    3.104a God *bless* you.

    3.105a Long *live* the King.

These wishes may also be stated with the modal *may*:

    3.104b *May* God *bless* you.

    3.105b *May* the King *live* long.

SUMMARY

We can summarize the distinctions among the various moods and tenses with a few example sentences:

    3.106a If she *owned* a car, she *would give* us a ride. (past subjunctive)

    b If she *had owned* a car, she *would have given* us a ride. (perfect subjunctive)

    c Since she *owns* a car, she *will give* us a ride. (indicative mood, present and future tenses, respectively)

    d Since she *owned* a car, she *gave* us a ride. (indicative mood, past tense)

    3.107a I know that you always *answer* letters promptly. (indicative mood, present tense)

    b I suggest that you *answer* this letter promptly. (present subjunctive)

    c Please *answer* the letter promptly. (imperative mood)

EXERCISES

A. Draw a chart like the one given below and enter each word from the verb phrase in the appropriate column. Do nothing with the other elements of the sentence.

example: We had been running for over an hour.

Modal	Have	Be	Verb
—	had	been	running

   1. Harriet was writing a novel.
   2. That faucet has been leaking for two days.
   3. You must have been the last one.
   4. They should have been sleeping.
   5. The hawk flew out of sight.
   6. The troops have arrived.
   7. The dog might have been hiding from us.
   8. He can have the money.
   9. They could have traded the car.
 10. We shall be waiting here.

B. Arrange the words from each of the following sentences in a chart like the one below:

Subject	Verb	Complement	Adverbial
Wanda	was reading	a book *(d.o.)*	at school *(place)*

   1. The neighbors have bought a motorcycle.
   2. Those remarks seem perfectly ridiculous.
   3. The building would have collapsed some time.
   4. That dog has grown more friendly recently.
   5. We are selling our car impulsively.
   6. Freddie wrote a check.
   7. Those men must have been cousins.

8. My tailor has become a new person.
9. My tailor has made a new suit.
10. Mark will build it outside.

C. Explain why these sentences are not possible:

1. *We washed the windows tomorrow.
2. *After we had found the mistake, we correct it.
3. *Last December she practices every day.
4. *Barbara claps her hands when she saw the doll.
5. *He will thank you after you had helped him.
6. *He was typing a letter when Annette has entered the room.
7. *Since you have been so nasty, I had not given you a birthday present.
8. *If you should go, I am sad.
9. *The Smiths will be packing their suitcases when you have seen them.
10. *Napoleon has died in 1821.

D. Fill in the blank with each of the modals: *may, might, can, could, will, would, shall, should, must*. How do the nine versions differ in meaning?
Joan _____ play the piano.

E. Each of the following sentences has more than one meaning, depending upon how we interpret the modal. Give each of these meanings.

1. You might know that he is not able to add.
2. You will answer the questions correctly.
3. That must be our classroom.
4. He may go to bed early tonight.
5. John could play the violin.
6. You can go to the devil.
7. She would wear her oldest dress to the party.
8. We should be happy to go with you.

F. Why do many people prefer the second sentence to the first one?

1. An example of an article would be *the*.
2. An example of an article is *the*.

G. Fill in the blank of each sentence with the standard past tense or past participle of the verb in parentheses. If you are in doubt about which form is used in standard English, consult a good dictionary; do not just guess.

  1. She _____ the horn at me. (blow)
  2. They have already _____ all the coffee. (drink)
  3. We _____ down to rest for a few minutes. (lie)
  4. They _____ their coats on the bed. (lay)
  5. He _____ about where he had been. (lie)
  6. The children _____ in the yard. (swing)
  7. The criminal has probably _____ away by now. (get)
  8. You should have _____ under the dryer. (sit)
  9. They must have _____ the baby down on the bed. (set)
  10. He _____ another piece of cake. (take)
  11. They have _____ away. (fly)
  12. This shirt _____ when I washed it. (shrink)
  13. The shoe _____ me perfectly. (fit)
  14. We had _____ before we heard the news. (rise)
  15. We had _____ our arms before we heard the news. (raise)
  16. Sarah has _____ her job again. (quit)
  17. Something _____ in the store. (stink)
  18. They have _____ often in the lake. (swim)
  19. They had already _____ the prisoner. (hang)
  20. The water pipes have _____. (burst)
  21. He _____ into the river. (dive)
  22. The noise _____ me very early this morning. (wake)
  23. We _____ to do better. (strive)
  24. She _____ her shoes under the bed. (fling)
  25. We have _____ our point. (prove)

H. Write interesting sentences using the verbs in the requested tenses:

  1. *mutilate*, past progressive
  2. *sneak*, past
  3. *decimate*, present progressive
  4. *lie* ("recline"), present perfect
  5. *switch off*, future

6. *swim*, future perfect
7. *hug*, present progressive
8. *swell*, past
9. *spill over*, future progressive
10. *hang* ("execute"), present perfect
11. *terminate*, future progressive
12. *be*, future
13. *prove*, past perfect
14. *chew out*, present progressive
15. *inundate*, present perfect progressive

I. Give the tense of each verb and explain why that tense is appropriate:

1. When he returned from the war, he learned that everything had changed.
2. As he was starting the car, he noticed a peculiar noise.
3. Your children are noisy.
4. Gerald will certainly mail the letter when you have finished it.
5. He has been treasurer for ten years.
6. He was treasurer for ten years.
7. He will be treasurer for ten years.
8. Peggy said, "I saw him on Tuesday."
9. Peggy said that she had seen him on Tuesday.
10. Hamlet kills Polonius, who has made a noise.
11. I worked while you were sleeping.
12. My experience in the kitchen was thrilling, but the food was unappetizing.

chapter 4 ━━━━━━━━

Passives

Although normal word order is SVO, we sometimes vary this arrangement to form questions, to emphasize certain words, or to provide variety. One means of giving prominence to a word is to place it first in the sentence:

4.1 *Yesterday* he was all right.

We sometimes move objects to the beginning, just as we do adverbials:

4.2 *That* you must never do again!
4.3 *This one* I especially like.

These fronted objects have extra stress placed on them when the sentences are spoken.

PASSIVES WITH *BE*

At times we cannot move the object to the beginning of the sentence:

4.4 Audrey chose Peter.

If we fronted the object as we did in **4.2** and **4.3**, we would obtain the unacceptable:

4.5 *Peter Audrey chose.

Yet we do have a structure known as the **passive** that permits us to place the receiver of the action first:

4.6 Peter was chosen by Audrey.

We understand this sentence to mean the same as the **active 4.4**, namely that Audrey did the choosing and that Peter was the one chosen.

Let us see how we revised **4.4** to produce **4.6**, both repeated here:

4.4 Audrey chose Peter.
4.6 Peter was chosen by Audrey.

First of all, the nouns have been interchanged. The one that occurs before the verb in **4.4** (*Audrey*) is after it in **4.6**, and the one after the verb in **4.4** (*Peter*) is in front of it in **4.6**. If we switch the nouns in **4.4**, we derive the following:

4.7 Peter   chose   Audrey.

But this by itself is not what we want because it yields the wrong meaning. We notice next that *by* appears in the passive sentence. Let us place it before *Audrey:*

4.8 Peter   chose   by Audrey.

This is still not enough to produce a passive sentence. We must do something to the verb. We may ask what is the difference between *chose* and *was chosen*. Both contain *choose*, and both sentences are in past tense. The passive also contains *was*, the past tense of *be*. Instead of the present participle that we are accustomed to seeing after the auxiliary *be* (*He was choosing*), we find the past participle, *was chosen*. Now if we add *be* and make the word after it a past participle, we can change **4.8** into the following:

4.9   Peter   was chosen   by Audrey.

This sentence is what we are trying to produce.

Let us go through the steps for forming the passive with another sentence:

4.10   The rat ate the cheese.

First we interchange the noun phrases:

4.11   The cheese   ate   the rat.

Next we insert *by:*

4.12   The cheese   ate   by the rat.

Finally we add *be* and make the main verb a past participle:

4.13   The cheese   was eaten   by the rat.

We recognize this sentence as synonymous with the active sentence **4.10**. In both, the rat did the eating and the cheese is that which was eaten.

So far we have seen only sentences with a main verb and no auxiliaries. We now should consider the position of the passive *be* when other auxiliaries are present.

4.14a   The director has forgotten the letter.
   b   The letter has been forgotten by the director.

As we can see, the passive *be* follows the auxiliary *have*. Here are some examples with other auxiliaries:

4.15a   The valedictorian should deliver the address.
   b   The address should be delivered by the valedictorian.
4.16a   The nurse was bathing the baby.
   b   The baby was being bathed by the nurse.
4.17a   An imbecile must have written this letter.
   b   This letter must have been written by an imbecile.

In each pair of sentences we see the noun phrases interchanged and *by* added in the passive versions. The passive *be* follows all other auxiliaries, and the word after it is a past participle (*delivered, bathed, written*). The form of the passive *be* is determined in each case by the auxiliary that precedes it: the infinitive *be* after a modal (**4.15**), the present participle *being* after *be* (**4.16**), and the past participle *been* (**4.17**) after *have*. Notice that both active and passive versions have the same meaning, including that provided by the auxiliaries. If one is progressive, so is the other, and so on.

Although many combinations of auxiliaries are possible in the passive, a few are not, namely those combinations of the progressive *be* preceded by *have* or a modal:

4.18a The dog has been chasing Michael.
 b *Michael has been being chased by the dog.
4.19a The owners should be washing the windows.
 b *The windows should be being washed by the owners.
4.20a That man must have been watching our house.
 b *Our house must have been being watched by that man.

Other combinations of auxiliaries occur freely in the passive, as we saw in **4.14–4.17**.

Only sentences with direct objects may be converted into passives. Hence, there is no passive for sentences with intransitive verbs:

4.21a The smoke vanished.
 b *Was vanished by the smoke.
4.22a The noise is subsiding.
 b *Is being subsided by the noise.

Nor do sentences with predicate nouns become passives:

4.23a Al has become a nuisance.
 b *A nuisance has been become by Al.
4.24a The guest of honor remained my bridge partner.
 b *My bridge partner was remained by the guest of honor.

Also, if a verb is followed by an adverbial noun rather than a direct object, the passive is not possible:

> **4.25a** Someone stupid must have weighed that package.
>
> **4.26a** The package must have weighed ten pounds.

In **4.25a**, *weigh* names an action and is followed by a direct object, but in **4.26a** it names a state and has an adverbial noun after it. Let us try converting the two sentences into the passive:

> **4.25b** That package must have been weighed by someone stupid.
>
> **4.26b** *Ten pounds must have been weighed by the package.

The sentence with an adverbial noun and no direct object, **4.26**, does not permit the passive. It is obvious from the **b** versions of **4.21–4.26** that only sentences with direct objects may become passives.

There are also a few transitive verbs that do not form passives, as seen in these examples:

> **4.27a** This weather suits me.
>
> **b** *I am suited by this weather.
>
> **4.28a** Carol resembles Aunt Peggy.
>
> **b** *Aunt Peggy is resembled by Carol.

Other verbs that block the passive, at least for certain meanings, include *have, involve, marry, form, want,* and a few more.

In addition to some verbs that have only active versions, such as those in the preceding paragraph, there are a few that have only passive forms:

> **4.29** It was *rumored* that he had been found.
>
> **4.30** They are *alleged* to have been witnesses.
>
> **4.31** Janice was *born* in Montreal.

It is pointless to try to provide active counterparts for these sentences.

At times the subject in the active sentence is an indefinite pronoun, as in the following:

4.32a Someone has stabbed the barber.

b The barber has been stabbed by someone.

We usually delete the *by* phrase in passives such as this, giving:

4.32c The barber has been stabbed.

We no longer have the *by* phrase to mark the sentence as a passive, but we do have *be* plus a past participle (*stabbed*). Here are some other examples of deleted *by* phrases:

4.33a Something is mashing me.

b I'm being mashed by something.

c I'm being mashed.

4.34a Someone pushed him.

b He was pushed by someone.

c He was pushed.

If the subject of the active sentence is not an indefinite pronoun such as *someone* or *something*, it usually cannot be deleted:

4.35a Randy pushed him.

b He was pushed by Randy.

If we deleted *by Randy*, we would lose information. We understand *He was pushed* to be equivalent to *He was pushed by someone*, as in **4.34**.

There is one other case in which the *by* phrase may be deleted—when the meaning of the verb is such that only one performer of the action is likely:

4.36a The jury found the defendant guilty.

b The defendant was found guilty by the jury.

c The defendant was found guilty.

4.37a A policeman has arrested Rhoda.

b Rhoda has been arrested by a policeman.

c Rhoda has been arrested.

It is only in sentences such as these that a noun phrase other than an indefinite pronoun may be deleted.

PAST PARTICIPLES AND ADJECTIVES

Some sentences admit two separate readings, depending upon how we interpret the word following *be:*

4.38   The door was closed.

This sentence may describe an action or a state. If we add other words after *closed* or compare the sentence with its opposite with *open/opened*, the ambiguity becomes obvious. When we talk about an action, we are free to add manner adverbials:

4.39   The door was closed suddenly.
4.40   The door was opened suddenly.

With the stative meaning we can use an adverbial of duration:

4.41   The door was closed throughout the performance.
4.42   The door was open throughout the performance.

Although some people consider both **4.39** and **4.41** passive sentences, there are two problems with such a classification. First, if **4.41** is a passive, it seems that **4.42** should be also; yet *open* is clearly an adjective, not a past participle. Apart from the *-ed* ending on *closed* and our knowledge that it is etymologically related to the verb *close*, there is no reason to consider **4.41** a passive; in fact, it is closer to **4.42** than to **4.39**. Second, if **4.41** is a passive, it must have a deleted *by* phrase and a corresponding active version, yet neither of the following is possible:

4.43a   *The door was closed throughout the performance by someone.
    b   *Someone closed the door throughout the performance.

Instead of calling *closed* in **4.41** a past participle, we will call it an adjective, the same as *open*. Its resemblance to the passive verb phrase *was closed* is a matter of etymological interest only.

To recapitulate, let us look at *broken:*

4.44a   The window was broken.
    b   The window was broken all winter.
    c   The window was broken intentionally.

The **a** version is ambiguous; the other two are not, **b** naming a state and **c** an action. If we consider **b** a sentence with a linking verb and a predicate adjective (*broken*), we can account for the absence of the following:

> **4.44d** *The window was broken by hail all winter.
> **e** *Hail broke the window all winter.

Since **4.44b** is not a passive, there is no reason to expect the **d** and **e** versions. We could substitute an adjective such as *dirty* for *broken* in this sentence and have the same structure. On the other hand, **c** is a passive, and we do have a corresponding active:

> **4.44f** Someone broke the window intentionally.

By calling *broken* an adjective in **4.44b** and a past participle in **4.44c**, we can account for the ambiguity of **4.44a**.

PASSIVES WITH *GET*

In addition to passives formed with the auxiliary *be*, there are those formed with *get:*

> **4.45a** Something bit John.
> **b** John was bitten.
> **c** John got bitten.

The passive with *get* occurs frequently in spoken English and in some informal writing, but it is rarely found in formal writing.
   Like *be, get* can also be a linking verb:

> **4.46** Caleb was sick.
> **4.47** Caleb got sick.

The meaning of *get* in **4.47** is very close to that of *become*. There are also several additional meanings of *get*, as we can see from the following examples:

> **4.48** They got to worrying about it.
> **4.49** They have got to go.

4.50   They've got a new car.

4.51   They got up.

4.52   They got the message.

4.53   He got his nose out of joint.

We will be concerned only with the passive meaning.

Because *get* has more meaning than *be* in some uses, such as **4.48–4.53**, there is a tendency to expect a difference in meaning between passives with *be* and those with *get*. In some sentences we may see such a difference:

4.54   Cathy was arrested.

4.55   Cathy got arrested.

We feel in **4.55** that Cathy was in some way responsible for the arrest; that is, it has the following meaning:

4.56   Cathy got herself arrested.

Passives with *be* do not permit reflexives such as *herself:*

4.57   *Cathy was herself arrested.

It would be tempting to say that passives with *be* make no statements about responsibility, but those with *get* do. However, such a generalization would be inaccurate because passives with *get* usually have two meanings, one that indicates responsibility and one that does not:

4.58a   Cathy got arrested through no fault of her own.

4.59a   Cathy got arrested on purpose.

Note that **4.59** permits the insertion of *herself*, but **4.58** does not:

4.58b   *Cathy got herself arrested through no fault of her own.

4.59b   Cathy got herself arrested on purpose.

Whenever responsibility on the part of the subject is intended, a reflexive pronoun (*herself, themselves, myself,* etc.) is either expressed or understood.

In some sentences the meaning with the reflexive is unlikely but remotely possible:

> **4.60a** I got caught in traffic.
>
> **b** ?I got myself caught in traffic.
>
> **4.61a** We got rained on.
>
> **b** ?We got ourselves rained on.
>
> **4.62a** Eloise finally got paid.
>
> **b** ?Eloise finally got herself paid.

The question mark means that we did not want to indicate that the **b** sentences are impossible (although **4.62b** may be), as would be the case if we had used an asterisk; yet we wanted to show that they are questionable.

We can, therefore, state the difference in meaning between passives with *be* and those with *get* as follows: Those with *be* make no statement about whether the subject is responsible for the action or not. Passives with *get* are ambiguous, having either the same neutral meaning as those with *be* or implying responsibility on the part of the subject. This ambiguity may be removed with the use of a reflexive pronoun or with certain adverbials (e.g., *through no fault of her own*).

Turning from meaning to form, we see that both passive auxiliaries are followed by past participles:

> **4.63** Herbert was *chosen*.
>
> **4.64** Herbert got *chosen*.

Also, both follow all other auxiliaries:

> **4.65** You might have *been* killed.
>
> **4.66** You might have *got* killed.

Yet there are some differences. First of all, adverbs are not positioned in the same place with the two passive auxiliaries:

> **4.67a** We finally were noticed.
>
> **b** We were finally noticed.
>
> **4.68a** We finally got noticed.
>
> **b** *We got finally noticed.

Some people may have stylistic preferences for positioning adverbs with *be*, choosing **4.67a** or **4.67b**; however, there is no freedom with *get*.

Second, in questions *be* is moved before the subject if it is the first auxiliary:

> **4.69a** They were erased.
>
> **b** Were they erased?

Questions with *get* are formed in the same manner as those with verbs other than *be:*

> **4.70a** They got erased.
>
> **b** *Got they erased?
>
> **c** Did they get erased?

The same pattern can be found with negatives:

> **4.71a** They were erased.
>
> **b** They were not erased.

Not follows *be*. With other verbs, *do* support is required:

> **4.72a** Sheila sneezed.
>
> **b** *Sheila sneezed not.
>
> **c** Sheila didn't sneeze.

Passives with *get* form negatives in the same way:

> **4.73a** They got erased.
>
> **b** *They got not erased.
>
> **c** They didn't get erased.

With questions, negatives, and similar structures, then, the passive auxiliary *get* does not function like *be*, but rather like other verbs.

WHY USE THE PASSIVE?

Grammar texts frequently caution students against using the passive, saying that it is less direct than the active and citing examples such as the following:

4.74a The book was read by me.
4.75a A good time was had by everyone.

These sentences would clearly be better as actives:

4.74b I read the book.
4.75b Everyone had a good time.

Examples such as these are unfortunate because they represent only restricted types of passives, not the full range. In particular, when the subject of an active sentence is a first-person pronoun (*I*, *we*), passives are rarely acceptable unless heavy stress is placed on the object of *by:*

4.76 The wall was painted by *us*, not by *them*.

Sentence **4.74a** is objectionable not just because it is a passive, but because it belongs to the subclass in which the object of *by* is *me* or *us*. Similarly, **4.75a** is unfortunate because it is trite and because this is one of the few instances in which *have* permits a passive; it normally functions like *weigh*, *measure*, and other stative verbs that we discussed earlier in this chapter.

When we examine books and articles written by distinguished authors, we do not find sentences like **4.74a** and **4.75a**, but we do find certain types of passives used rather frequently.

The following directions cover the most frequent uses of the passive:

1. Use the passive if the agent is unimportant, unknown, or not easily stated.

   Weak: Someone murdered Cora last night. (active)
   Improved: Cora was murdered last night. (passive)

   Weak: Something or someone has hit me. (active)
   Improved: I've been hit. (passive)

   Weak: Something drowned him in the river. (active)
   Improved: He was drowned in the river. (passive)

2. Use the passive if you wish to suppress the agent for reasons of tact or scholarly objectivity.

   Blunt: Many people believe that you did not handle the latest crisis well. (active)

Tactful: Many people believe that the latest crisis was not handled well. (passive)

Blunt: We now invite you to visit our garden. (active)
Tactful: You are now invited to visit our garden. (passive)

Personal: We call each object of a set a member of the set.
Objective: Each object of a set is called a member of the set.

3. Use the passive to emphasize the patient rather than the agent.

   Agent emphasized: A car has run over your cat. (active)
   Patient emphasized: Your cat has been run over by a car. (passive)

   Agent emphasized: The cheering crowds encouraged the President. (active)
   Patient emphasized: The President was encouraged by the cheering crowds. (passive)

4. Use the passive to prevent vague pronoun reference.

   Vague: They told me that you are hiring part-time employees. (active)
   Improved: I was told that you are hiring part-time employees. (passive)

5. Use the passive if the agent is extremely long.

   Confusing: A man in a stocking mask who threatened to kill an elderly woman if she did not open the safe shot her yesterday. (active)
   Clear: An elderly woman was shot yesterday by a man in a stocking mask who threatened to kill her if she did not open the safe.

6. Use the passive to avoid the pronouns *one* and *you* if the context makes these words inappropriate.

   Too formal: One can find these books on the third level.
   Too informal: You can find these books on the third level. (if *you* is the indefinite pronoun meaning "a person")
   Neutral: These books can be found on the third level.

Most of the conditions under which the passive is better than the active are found primarily in formal writing. For this reason, you will find many more passives in scientific writing or in essays on literary criticism than you will in fiction or other informal writing.

EXERCISES

A. The **b** sentences below are intended as passive counterparts of the **a** sentences, but some are unsatisfactory because a change other than that needed to form the passive was made. Locate the passives that are incorrect, explain what is wrong, and correct them.

    1a. The attendant has already parked your car.
      b. Your car had already been parked by the attendant.
    2a. An odious person was whistling a patriotic tune.
      b. A patriotic tune was whistled by an odious person.
    3a. Janice must have noticed the dripping faucet.
      b. The dripping faucet must have been noticed by Janice.
    4a. The dog was digging a hole.
      b. A hole was being dug by the dog.
    5a. The passengers could hear the pilot's announcement.
      b. The pilot's announcement could have been heard by the passengers.

B. Convert the following sentences into passives, deleting the *by* phrase wherever possible:

    1. Someone has found a bomb in the basement.
    2. People can't trust him.
    3. Olivia drove the bus.
    4. Someone must have found him by now.
    5. The referee was attacking Gwendolyn.
    6. The auditor has carefully audited your account.
    7. The judge pronounced the sentence.
    8. Judge Bates pronounced the sentence.
    9. Someone has called the wrong number.
    10. Her parents reared her in South America.

C. Some words can be either adjectives or past participles, such as *closed* and *broken*. Others are only one of these. Create sentences like *The door was closed* for the following words and classify them as: (1) either participle or adjective, (2) only participle, or (3) only adjective.

1. embarrassed	6. shut	11. disheveled
2. elated	7. amazed	12. amused
3. paid	8. married	13. degraded
4. inspired	9. caught	14. stricken
5. named	10. concerned	15. dedicated

Add ten additional words and follow the same directions.

D. Convert the active sentences to passives and the passives to actives. Delete the *by* phrase in the passive whenever possible. Decide which version is better in each case and try to explain why.

1. Albert loves Wanda.
2. Hank must have been questioned by the teacher.
3. The building is cooled by central air conditioning.
4. Lightning struck the tree.
5. The window was closed by me.
6. Someone left the lights on all night.
7. The detective got shot.
8. Barbara could smell the cabbage.
9. You've been had.
10. Evelyn got caught by the teacher.
11. Someone must clean everything today.
12. That book can be found on the third level of the stacks.
13. This acrobatic team is admired all over the world.
14. I was reared in New England.
15. The window washer saw a strange sight.
16. In 1945 the allied powers defeated Germany.
17. Everyone signed the birthday card.
18. She was obsessed by a strange notion.
19. Tony wrote a poem.
20. The piano tuner tuned the piano today.

E. Draw a chart with four columns: Subject, Verb, Complement, and Adverbial. Then write the words from the following sentences in the proper columns and classify the complements and adverbials.

1. The salespeople were watching the customer.
2. He got nasty after his sixteenth drink.
3. Brenda felt ashamed.
4. I painted all morning.
5. His friends were broken-hearted.
6. My glasses got broken.
7. His arm was bent at the elbow.
8. Her card was bent accidentally.
9. The plant grew fast last year.
10. The plant grew tall in the greenhouse.
11. He grew tomatoes.
12. The pupil was reading aloud.
13. That story was exciting.
14. The child was exciting the animals.
15. The Andersons are divorced.
16. Carla was divorced by her husband.
17. She slept in the living room.
18. It will turn cold tonight.
19. Everything must be approached with care.
20. He was a roughneck all summer.

chapter 5 ═══════════

The Noun Phrase

As we examined sentences in the preceding chapters, we frequently mentioned noun phrases and their functions as subjects, objects, predicate nouns, and objects of prepositions:

5.1 *Those shoes* are new. (subject)

5.2 The cowboy roped *the steer*. (direct object)

5.3 Your sister is *a pest*. (predicate noun)

5.4 I sent the check to *the bank*. (object of a preposition)

The objects of certain prepositions can be converted into indirect objects:

5.5a I signaled the answer to *Bob*.

b I signaled *Bob* the answer.

In a passive sentence we rearrange the subject and object noun phrases:

5.6a A rattlesnake bit Carolyn.

b Carolyn was bitten by a rattlesnake.

Because it is only by its use in a sentence that we can classify a word as a noun or any other part of speech, we have devoted the first four chapters of this book to the study of functions. It is now time to look more closely at the noun phrase, the structure that performs the functions we have been discussing.

UNIQUE NOUNS AND NAMES OF CLASSES

We can speak or write about specific items or about members of classes. One means of doing this is to use a **proper noun** to name a specific person or place and a **common noun** for a class. For example, the common noun *country* applies to several hundred national units; if we wish to designate one member of this class, we use a proper noun such as *Germany, Nigeria, Peru, Mexico, India,* or *Japan*. We can list a few other examples:

Common Noun	Proper Nouns
city	Rome, Istanbul, Sidney, Cairo, Caracas
county	Kent, Washtenaw, Marin, Yoknapatawpha
university	Oxford, Sorbonne, Stanford, Princeton
planet	Mars, Jupiter, Mercury, Saturn
river	Seine, Amazon, Yangtze, Guadalquivir
state	Vermont, Ohio, Tennessee, Utah
woman	Beth, Ms. Hopkins, Aunt Julia

A common noun refers to a number of people or objects with similar characteristics; a proper noun refers to one that is unique.

If we considered all people, places, and things in the world, we would find several with the same names. There are probably thousands of males named *Robert*, and some names of cities are not restricted to one location (e.g., *Springfield, Portland, New London, San Juan*). Yet the context is usually such that only one person or place is likely. If the mother of a boy named Robert asks her husband, "Where is Robert?" he does not think she means Robert Redford or Robert Goulet. Nor are people living near Springfield, Illinois, confused upon hearing that a neighbor has "gone to Springfield for the day"; they do not think the speaker means Springfield, Missouri. In case the meaning is not clear from the context, we add other details, such as *Portland, Oregon*. Names like *Robert, Portland,* and *Springfield* are proper nouns that designate people or places unique within a given context.

Although common nouns name classes rather than individual items, we have ways of making them designate a specific member of the class without giving them proper names. In a restaurant we may order "a steak," meaning any member of the class of meats called *steak*. Once we have made the order, we are no longer concerned with just any steak, but with a particular one. If we call the waiter back and mention our order, we do not use sentences like the following:

> **5.7a** When will a steak be ready?
>
> **5.8a** I forgot to tell you that I would like a steak well done.

Once we have singled out a specific member of the class, we stop referring to it with the article *a* or *an* and switch to *the:*

> **5.7b** When will the steak be ready?
>
> **5.8b** I forgot to tell you that I would like the steak well done.

As long as we mean any member of the class, we continue using *a* or *an;* to designate a specific one that has been identified, we use *the*.

At times shared knowledge permits us to use *the* on the first mentioning of an object. For example, joint owners of a car would understand

> **5.9** Are you taking the car?

Also, under specific circumstances, the following would be clear:

> **5.10** Have you seen the play yet?
>
> **5.11** Where did the batter go?
>
> **5.12** What happened to the radio?

Since we know how many suns are visible from the earth and how many devils certain religions recognize, we may say the following:

> **5.13** The sun rose at 6:45 this morning.
>
> **5.14** He is not afraid of the devil.

These words are still common nouns, but they are specifically identified with *the*.

The usual term for *a* is **indefinite article**, and that for *the* is **definite article**. There are also **demonstratives**, which indicate a definite object just as *the* does. They also provide additional information, as we can see from these examples:

5.15 *This* tulip came from Holland.

5.16 *These* apples are rotten.

5.17 I like *that* song.

5.18 She handed *those* children the passes.

Although we do not necessarily point our fingers or nod our heads at the objects named when we use the demonstratives, we do so mentally. As we can tell from the examples, *this* and its plural *these* are used for objects that are near; *that* and the plural *those* are for those farther away.

An alternative to *a* is a number, either specific (*six, five, a thousand*) or general (*many, some, several, a few*). Like *a*, we do not continue using numbers by themselves after the first occurrence:

5.19a He handed me six oranges and some cucumbers. *Six oranges were sour, but some cucumbers were good.

b He handed me six oranges and some cucumbers. The oranges were sour, but the cucumbers were good.

c He handed me six oranges and some cucumbers. The six oranges were sour, but the cucumbers were good.

If we want to continue using the number, we must also use *the* or one of the demonstratives. We have this same option with the indefinite article *a*, but we must make a change:

5.20a In the refrigerator were an orange, an apple, and three bananas. *We shared an orange.

b In the refrigerator were an orange, an apple, and three bananas. We shared the orange.

c In the refrigerator were an orange, an apple, and three bananas. We shared the one orange.

Here we are not permitted to continue using *an*, but we may convert it to the etymologically related *one* and add *the*.

POSSESSIVES

In addition to articles and demonstratives, possessives are used to make common nouns refer to specific members of their class:

> **5.21**   *Harold's* horse is getting too fat.
>
> **5.22**   We mailed *Abner's* grandmother some persimmons.
>
> **5.23**   That is *the cat's* bowl.
>
> **5.24**   The court has appointed us *your* guardian.
>
> **5.25**   The dog chased *its* tail.

In each example the possessive not only identifies the noun it modifies, but it also gives additional information in the way that demonstratives both identify and point out. This other information may be ownership:

> **5.26**   *The woman's* purse was stolen.
>
> **5.27**   Do you like *my* car?

At other times possession refers to parts of the body or qualities that we do not "own":

> **5.28**   The man raised *his* arm.
>
> **5.29**   *Marie's* intelligence is astounding.

Other possessives indicate the origin of the noun:

> **5.30**   *The sun's* rays are bright.

Still others have a relationship with nouns similar to that of subject and verb or verb and object:

> **5.31**   *Their* hatred for each other was horrifying. (Cf. They hated each other.)
>
> **5.32**   She barely escaped from *her* pursuers. (Cf. People pursued her.)

And there are a variety of other relationships between the possessive and the noun it modifies: *a day's work* (measure), *actors' directions* (directions for actors), and the like. A sentence like the following can have several meanings:

5.33 Have you seen *my* painting?

Does *my painting* mean one that I own, one that I made, or one that was made of me? Since ownership is only one of many relationships between possessives and the nouns they modify, the word *possessive* may not be the best one. Other terms, such as *genitive*, are equally unsatisfactory, and no one has suggested anything better. Because of its widespread use, we shall continue to use *possessive*, noting its deficiencies.

In some ways possessives are like articles and demonstratives. As we have already noticed, all three can be used to designate a particular item. They are also mutually exclusive because a noun may be modified by only one of these words. We cannot, for example, combine an article and a demonstrative (*the those cookies, *that the ruby), an article and a possessive (*the Bill's house, *Bill's the house), or a demonstrative and a possessive (*this his rug, *her those socks). It may appear that a combination such as *this boy's dog* is an exception to the preceding observation, but we can readily show that *this* relates to *boy's*, not *dog*. We are pointing out the boy, not the dog. Also, if we change the number of either noun, *this* changes to *these* only if *boy's* is affected: *this boy's dogs, these boys' dogs, these boys' dog*. Another similarity among possessives, articles, and demonstratives is that singular nouns that can be counted must be preceded by one of these modifiers:

5.34a *Car* is in *garage*.

We can say "one car, two cars, three cars" and "one garage, two garages, three garages." Nouns that name masses (*air, water, oil*) and a few others (*furniture*) are not counted, and they can be used without modifiers (*He tried to mix oil and water together*). Those that can be counted must be modified when they are singular, as we can see from **5.34a**. An adjective alone is not sufficient for making the sentence acceptable:

5.34b *Green car is in big garage.

However, an article, a demonstrative, or a possessive does make the sentence complete:

5.34c *The* car is in *that* garage.
   d *My* car is in *your* garage.

Possessives are in many ways like articles and demonstratives.

But there are differences as well. The article *the* has the meaning "specific" and little else. The demonstratives include the meaning "specific" and also the notions of nearness and number (singular or plural). The possessives, by contrast, contain in addition to the notion of "specific" the full meaning of a noun or pronoun. In the following sentences we can illustrate these differences in meaning:

    5.35a *The* coat fell to the floor.

       b *That* coat fell to the floor.

       c *Cynthia's* coat fell to the floor.

Possessives have more meaning than articles and demonstratives.

Also, possessives are noun phrases in themselves, whereas articles and demonstratives only modify nouns; that is, like other nouns, possessives are singular or plural:

    5.36a He found *the woman's* money. (singular)

       b He found *the women's* money. (plural)

Possessives may be modified by articles, demonstratives, other possessives, and adjectives:

    5.37a He thanked *the children's* grandmother. (modified by the article *the*)

       b He thanked *those children's* grandmother. (modified by the demonstrative *those*)

       c He thanked *our children's* grandmother. (modified by the possessive *our*)

       d He thanked *the unruly children's* grandmother. (modified by the adjective *unruly* and the article *the*)

Possessives can be modified by most of the structures that go with other nouns.

As noun phrases, possessives may be replaced with pronouns:

    5.38a *The tall boy's* glasses are broken.

       b *His* glasses are broken.

    5.39a We were grading *those students'* papers.

       b We were grading *their* papers.

We readily recognize *his* as meaning *the tall boy's* and *their* as referring to *those students'*.

Finally, possessives can usually be paraphrased with prepositional phrases:

    5.40a This is *my aunt's* friend.

       b This is a friend *of my aunt*.

    5.41a *The book's* cover is torn.

       b The cover *of the book* is torn.

Articles and demonstratives cannot be paraphrased in this way.

Possessives that precede the nouns they modify (e.g., *the book's, my*) are often called **inflected possessives;** those that appear in prepositional phrases are called **periphrastic possessives**. We usually use the inflected possessive for people and the periphrastic construction for nonhumans:

    5.42 *Helen's* new job is exciting.

    5.43 We need to replace the roof *of the barn*.

For this reason, we find the following sentence peculiar:

    5.44a The man who lives in the town's middle wrote something unkind on the page's bottom about the waist of Lucy.

We expect the possessives to be stated like this:

    5.44b The man who lives in the middle of town wrote something unkind on the bottom of the page about Lucy's waist.

That is, we do not expect the inflected possessive with the nonhuman nouns *middle* and *bottom*, but we do with the human noun *Lucy*.

However, there are other instances in which good writers depart from this customary practice. For example, we can find any of these:

    5.45a This is Nancy's picture.

       b This is a picture of Nancy.

       c This is a picture of Nancy's.

The **a** version is ambiguous, but **b** is not. The **c** version has only two meanings, as opposed to the three of **a**. Note that **c** has the inflected and the periphrastic formations combined. Other departures from the practice of using the inflected possessive for humans and the periphrastic for nonhumans can be seen in such structures as *the sun's rays*, *the dog's howl*, and *the car's tires*.

We usually find the periphrastic construction when the possessive noun phrase is long. We may feel comfortable with fairly short phrases such as **5.46a** and **5.47a**, but for longer ones we prefer the *of* phrase even for humans:

5.46a *The man on the street's* opinion is often odd.

   b The opinion *of the man on the street* is often odd.

5.47a *The people next door's* dog kept me awake all night.

   b The dog *of the people next door* kept me awake all night.

5.48a *The people who live next door to my sister's* junk-filled yard is an eyesore.

   b The junk-filled yard *of the people who live next door to my sister* is an eyesore.

Sentence **5.48a** illustrates one reason for preferring the periphrastic construction for long modifiers. Does the junk-filled yard belong to the people next door or to my sister? If the people live next door to my sister's junk-filled yard, we are saying. "The people is an eyesore," clearly an odd statement. A popular sentence of earlier grammarians was the following:

5.49 The daughter of Pharaoh's son is the son of Pharaoh's daughter.

At first reading, the meaning appears to be impossible. It is only when we realized that the possessive may relate to an entire phrase (*the daughter of Pharaoh*) as well as to a single word (*Pharaoh*) that the sentence makes sense.

Another potentially cumbersome structure is the sequence of possessives. There is usually no problem with one possessive modified by just one other:

5.50 *Maureen's husband's* cousin is a book salesman.

5.51 I accepted *my nephew's* suggestion.

5.52 *My wife's* grandfather was there.

But if we have more than two possessives in succession, the meaning becomes confusing:

> **5.53** My wife's first husband's only child's grandfather was there.

We could have extended the structure even further by letting it be the grandfather's nurse who was there, but the sentence is sufficiently confusing as it is.

Since many people hesitate over the written representation of inflected possessives, let us look at the rules for their formation:

1. For singular nouns, add an apostrophe and *s: girl* (singular), *girl's* (possessive); *Danny, Danny's*.
2. For plural nouns ending in *s*, add an apostrophe: *boys* (plural), *boys'* (possessive); *dentists, dentists'*.
3. For plural nouns not ending in *s*, add an apostrophe and *s: women* (plural), *women's* (possessive); *firemen, firemen's*.
4. Proper nouns not ending in *s* in the singular follow the same rules as common nouns: *Bob, Bob's* (singular); *Bobs, Bobs'* (plural).
5. Proper nouns ending in *s* in the singular may follow the same rules as other proper nouns: *Mr. Jones, Mr. Jones's* (singular); *the Joneses, the Joneses'* (plural). However, there is an option in that the singular possessive may be *Mr. Jones'*, the form that is normally used by people who pronounce it as one syllable.
6. Indefinite pronouns follow the same rules as nouns: *someone's, nobody's, something's, everyone's, no one's*.
7. Personal pronouns do not have an apostrophe: *yours, hers, his, ours, theirs, its*. The possessive *its* is distinguished from the contraction of *it is*, which is written *it's*.

ADJECTIVES

Instead of limiting a class by the use of an article, a demonstrative, or a possessive, we may use adjectives such as *loud, horrible, green*, or *slovenly*. For example, if we want to divide towns into subclasses, we have several means available: *small towns* or *large towns, ugly towns* or *pretty towns, backward towns* or *progressive towns*. In each subdivision we have somewhat arbitrarily created a dichotomy so that a town that does not belong in one category (e.g., *ugly*) belongs in the other (*pretty*). The criteria for placing a town in one category or the other may be entirely subjective, or they may be objective as in the case of size.

As we are making subdivisions of a set of objects, we are not limited to two categories. For example, we may have three divisions: *small, medium-sized,* and *large*. Or there may be four: *northern, eastern, southern,* and *western*. Depending upon our interests, we may segment the class however we choose. If our interests lie in nationalities, we may divide towns into *Mexican towns, Bulgarian towns, Chinese towns,* and so on, until we run out of countries. For other objects, we may make subdivisions according to colors, breaking the color spectrum at as many or as few places as we choose.

We can see the limiting function of adjectives in the following sentences:

5.54a My sister bought *a dog*.

b My sister bought *a huge dog*.

5.55a Harold has become *an editor*.

b Harold has become *an excellent editor*.

5.56a I consider him *a prude*.

b I consider him *a silly prude*.

5.57a We are buying *a car*.

b We are buying *a new car*.

In each of these sentences the adjective serves to limit the noun to a subclass of the set; in none of them does it make the noun one specific entity.

Often we use adjectives for their own sake, in which case they may be more important than the nouns they modify:

5.58a I have *an arm*.

b I have *a sore arm*.

5.59a That certainly is *a sunset*.

b That certainly is *a beautiful sunset*.

In these sentences the **a** versions are uninteresting because they give information that the listener or reader presumably knows. Although the adjectives in the **b** versions do serve to limit the class (sore vs. healthy arms, beautiful vs. unspectacular sunsets), our purpose is to comment on soreness or beauty, not to limit the nouns. It should not be assumed that the only reason we use adjectives is to restrict subclasses of nouns.

In addition to using different adjectives that contrast, such as *tall* and *short*, we sometimes speak of greater or lesser degrees: *tall, taller, tallest; delightful, more delightful, most delightful; friendly, less friendly, the least friendly.* Thus, if we consider two ropes to be short, we do not distinguish them if we say, "Bring me the short rope." We can say, "Bring me the *shorter* rope." Most adjectives of one syllable and some of two syllables take comparatives in *-er* and superlatives in *-est.* A number of adjectives with two syllables and most that are longer form comparisons with *more* and *most* or *less* and *least.*

At times we do not content ourselves with a single adjective to modify a noun but use two or more:

> **5.60** I had to read a *long, dull, complicated* article.
>
> **5.61** Those *tall, stately* trees are beautiful.

Whenever two or more adjectives can be interchanged (*dull, long, complicated* in **5.60**) or permit the placement of *and* between them (*tall and stately* in **5.61**), they are said to be **coordinate**, and we separate them with commas. Since articles, demonstratives, numbers, possessives, and adjectives are different kinds of modifiers, they do not permit rearrangement or the insertion of *and;* we, therefore, do not place commas between these types of modifiers, such as between *a* and *long* in **5.60** or between *those* and *tall* in **5.61**. In **5.62**, we see another kind of modifier that does not form a coordinate sequence:

> **5.62** He built a tall stone fence.

Because *stone* names the material of which the fence is made, it is different from *tall;* hence, there is no comma separating *tall* and *stone.* We could not say "a stone tall fence" or "a tall and stone fence."

Although adjectives are like articles, demonstratives, and possessives in that they may limit nouns, they are different from these other words:

1. Whereas adjectives may show comparison, the others do not (*happy, happier;* *this, thiser).

2. Although there may be several adjectives preceding a noun (*an old, helpless, gray dog*), not more than one member of the other classes may occur there (*my your books).

3. If a noun has an article, a demonstrative, or a possessive, the other two are prohibited. It is possible, however, to have one of these words and a following adjective (**the that rug; the new rug*).

4. When a noun has an article, a demonstrative, or a possessive as well as an adjective before it, the adjective follows the other word (*a blue flower,* **blue a flower; that naughty girl,* **naughty that girl*).

5. An adjective has more semantic content than an article or a demonstrative, and it restricts the noun to a subclass, not to a unique member.

6. A singular count noun must have an article, a demonstrative, or a possessive accompanying it (*The glass broke.* *Glass broke). An adjective will not fulfill this requirement (**Pretty glass broke*).

Some books refer to articles, demonstratives, possessives, and numbers as **determiners** to distinguish them from adjectives.

COMPOUNDS

The adjective plus noun construction looks very much like another with a slightly different meaning, the **compound:**

Compound	*Modifier + Noun*
a blackboard	a black board
a cold war	a cold glass
a redhead	a red head
a dumbwaiter	a dumb waiter
a grand piano	a large piano

We do not think of a *blackboard* as just any board that is black, as we do with the modifier-plus-noun construction. We recognize similar differences in the other pairs. Each of the modifier-plus-noun combinations can be paraphrased with "A _____ that is _____" as "A waiter that is dumb." The compounds do not permit this paraphrase. In addition, the modifier-plus-noun combinations can be altered by changing the adjective: *a black board, a green board, a yellow board;* the compounds do not permit such substitution. We also notice a difference in pronunciation. The heavier stress is on the second element, the noun, in the modifier-plus-noun constructions; in the compounds it is on the first element.

Let us look at a typical contrast:

5.63 We ate *a hot dog*.

5.64 We chased *a hot dog*.

In **5.63**, we are speaking of a wiener on a bun, and we would be upset if someone served us a hot dog made with dog meat. In **5.64**, we mean a canine that is hot. This difference in meaning is matched by the one in pronunciation that we mentioned in the last paragraph. For the food, we stress *hot* more than we do *dog;* for the animal we place heavier stress on *dog*.

Sometimes compounds are spelled as separate words, as we can see with *a hot dog, a cold war,* and *a grand piano*. Others are spelled without a space between their components: *hotbed, scarecrow, leapfrog, roommate, snapshot, housekeeper*. Still others are hyphenated: *mother-in-law, water-repellent, high-octane*. The usual progression is for a compound to start out spelled as two separate words (*basket ball*). It is later hyphenated (*basket-ball*), and finally it is written solid (*basketball*).

The meaning of a compound is often more restricted than that of an adjective plus noun. For example, *a black bird*, adjective plus noun meaning "bird that is black," restricts the class of birds to those of a single color, including crows, buzzards, and others. The compound *blackbird*, however, is a further restriction to one group of birds that are black. Similarly, a *sidewalk* is not just any walkway that goes to the side.

With *sidewalk* we see another feature of compounds. We tend to think of them as single units, not as two separate words, and we often lose track of their original meaning. For many sidewalks, the first component is not very meaningful; we, therefore, see nothing strange about a sidewalk that is placed in the middle of a yard. Similarly, we find nothing incongruous with eating *a cold hot dog*, taking an examination in *a pink bluebook*, or writing on *a green blackboard*.

Since compounds function as single words, we shall consider them as units, regardless of how they are spelled. The noun phrase *a small high chair* will, therefore, be said to consist of an article (*a*), an adjective (*small*), and a noun (*high chair*).

The semantic relationship between the parts of a compound can be any of several possibilities. *A bird dog* is a dog that hunts birds, but *birdseed* is a seed that birds eat. A *birdbath* is a bath for birds, and a *birdbrain* is a person with a brain like that of a bird. A *bird lover* is a person who loves birds, unless we are reading imaginative literature, in which case it may be a bird that is in love. Turning to other words, a *redhead* and a *blackhead* normally have nothing in common. Compounds with *horse* as the first element show an especially wide range of meanings: *horse show, horselaugh, horse doctor, horsetail, horse feed, horse breeder, horse race, horsefly, horse disease, horse opera,* and others. Many compounds with animal names as the first element show metaphoric comparisons: *an eagle eye, a catnap, a rat nest, rabbit ears, a cowlick, horse feathers, a wolf whistle, a sheepskin, a pigskin, a bear hug, the fox-trot.*

It is possible to expand compounds. For example, by combining *base* and *ball* we obtain *baseball.* If we add this to *club*, we get *baseball club.* A baseball club composed of amateurs is an *amateur baseball club.* If this club is in a small town, it is a *small-town amateur baseball club.* Other extended compounds include *a fifty-mile radius, volunteer fire department, weekend houseguest, double-barreled shotgun auction,* and the like. The fact that many of these are spelled as separate words makes them less obvious than they would be if we spelled them solid: *weekendhouseguest.* Even a cursory inspection of a daily newspaper or a current magazine will show many examples. As we said earlier, they function as single units and are not treated as modifier-plus-noun constructions.

EXERCISES

A. Replace each noun phrase in the following sentences with a pronoun:

 1. Those three wooly coats are Robert's.
 2. My generous aunt has given my money to that beggar.
 3. Where did the gray mother cat find her young kitten?
 4. Does your nephew like this dreadful city?
 5. That last ham sandwich tasted peculiar.

B. Replace the proper nouns with common nouns that refer to the same people or objects. You may use articles and possessives but no other modifiers. How is meaning affected with your substitutions?

 1. Brenda Farrell sailed on the *Queen Elizabeth* yesterday.
 2. In January we made an exciting trip to the Himalayas.

   3. The Statue of Liberty was a gift from France.
   4. When I read *The Heart of Midlothian* this time, Jeannie Deans seemed more stupid than ever.
   5. He will be staying at the St. Francis while he is in San Francisco.
   6. Mr. Pruitt assured Paul that the Xerox Corporation would be happy to send him the information he requested.
   7. Mother took a cab to Kennedy Airport.
   8. Does the Mississippi River flow through Louisiana?
   9. Do you like your new Mercury?
   10. He thought he saw the President crossing Pennsylvania Avenue.

C. Replace the common nouns with proper nouns:
   1. That planet is closer to our planet than this one is.
   2. Did the woman travel far up the river?
   3. One day last month my friend bought a car.
   4. I rode to a city on a train.
   5. That man has been talking to the devil.
   6. In the forest the outlaw has made his home.
   7. Was that man living in this county then?
   8. I flew from one continent to another continent in two hours.
   9. Is the bank open on this holiday?
   10. I was eating in a restaurant.

D. Use a definite article, a demonstrative, or a possessive to make each of the nouns in the following sentences more specific:
   1. A man was whistling a tune.
   2. A dog ran under a car.
   3. An uncle handed an attendant a key.
   4. Would you like pickles on a sandwich?
   5. A nurse became a friend.

E. Write the possessives of the following nouns and pronouns:

1. bird	7. man
2. birds	8. men
3. someone	9. they
4. he	10. grandfather
5. Louise Percy	11. Senator Sanders
6. no one	12. the Smiths

13. ox
14. Ray Pearce
15. sheep
16. it
17. Dr. Adams
18. Charles
19. you
20. who

F. Make the nouns in the following sentences more specific by adding adjectives. Some of your adjectives may be commonplace (*little, old, brown,* etc.), but the others should be more imaginative.

1. The woman suddenly skated to the window.
2. His teacher lives in that apartment.
3. This chair belongs in the room.
4. Some children were giggling hysterically at your shoes.
5. The speech did not interest the people.
6. That hotel looked welcome to the traveler.
7. This snow is upsetting your babysitter.
8. Where can a shopper find a carton of eggs in this store?
9. The witch hovered in the air.
10. The woman dropped crumbs on the floor.

G. On a sheet of paper draw three columns labeled *Noun, Adjective,* and *Adverb.* Place each of the words given below under the appropriate column, and add or remove suffixes to provide the other two forms. That is, if *stupid* were given, you would write it under the adjective column and then provide the adverb *stupidly* and the noun *stupidity.* If you were given *wretchedly,* you would write it under the adverb column and provide the noun *wretchedness* and the adjective *wretched.*

1. duty
2. accurately
3. carefully
4. kindness
5. zeal
6. beautiful
7. fatally
8. nervous
9. cruelty
10. rigidly

H. Write compounds using the following words as the last element. For some of them, use expanded compounds such as *weekend houseguest.*

1. door
2. window
3. man
4. truck
5. pen
6. paper
7. party
8. school
9. dress
10. club

chapter 6 ════════════

Clauses and Phrases
that Modify Nouns

In the last chapter we saw that there are several ways to designate
which member of a class we are indicating. One of these is to use
the definite article *the*, which shows that the object has been previously identified, either in an earlier statement or from shared
knowledge:

> **6.1** At the zoo we saw an orangutan and a baboon. *The*
> orangutan interested me more than *the* baboon did.
>
> **6.2** *The* principal will talk with you now.

Another way of specifying individuals is by pointing them out with
demonstratives:

> **6.3** *These* cookies are too sweet.
>
> **6.4** Who is *that* pest?

Possessives provide a third means:

> **6.5** *Our* clock must be fast.
>
> **6.6** Have you ridden in *Dick's* car?

Or we can use adjectives:

> **6.7** The teacher likes *inquisitive* children.
>
> **6.8** He went to the *new* courthouse.

In each of these sentences we are indicating either a specific member of the class (*that pest, Dick's car, the new courthouse*) or a subclass (*inquisitive children*).

In many sentences the modifier carries a meaning at least as important as that of the noun:

> **6.9a** He brought me some cherries.
>
> **b** He brought me some ripe cherries.
>
> **6.10a** Do you like poems?
>
> **b** Do you like my poems?
>
> **6.11a** We gave her some water.
>
> **b** We gave her some poisoned water.

But even for sentences such as these, the modifier still limits.

RELATIVE CLAUSES

Instead of defining an object by pointing it out, naming its characteristics, and the like, we often relate it to a specific event or state. For example, we may start with this sentence:

> **6.12** Lorraine was hit by *a car*.

If we want to indicate which car hit her, we may do so with the devices we have already considered (*that car, your car, an old car*). Or we may say something else about it:

> **6.13** The car was driven by a maniac.
>
> **6.14** The car was barely moving.

We can combine either sentence **6.13** or **6.14** with **6.12** and obtain the following:

> **6.15** Lorraine was hit by a car *that was driven by a maniac*.
>
> **6.16** Lorraine was hit by a car *that was barely moving*.

In each of these sentences we are limiting the class of cars by means of a structure that is known as a **relative clause**.

Relative clauses can be paraphrased with complete sentences, such as **6.13** and **6.14**, which contain an instance of the same noun as that modified (i.e., *car*). Here are some other examples:

> **6.17a** The bottle was empty. The bottle rolled down the aisle.
>
>   **b** The bottle *that rolled down the aisle* was empty.
>
> **6.18a** The man was angry. The man hit me.
>
>   **b** The man *who hit me* was angry.

In each case we decide which act or state is to be used for purposes of identification. In **6.17b**, we are stating that the bottle was empty and using the relative clause to tell the reader which bottle is meant. In **6.18b**, *who hit me* tells which man was angry. If the writer had had a different meaning in mind, the following sentences might have resulted:

> **6.17c** The bottle *that was empty* rolled down the aisle.
>
> **6.18c** The man *who was angry* hit me.

Now we are using the relative clauses to tell the reader which bottle rolled down the aisle and which man hit me. From pairs of sentences in isolation, such as **6.17a** and **6.18a**, there is usually no way to tell which is the more important and which is to serve an identifying function. If the sentences occur in a larger context and if we know the intent of the speaker or writer, however, there is only one choice. We say that the sentence which serves an identifying function is **subordinated** to the other one.

Relative clauses are generally introduced by the **relative pronouns** *who, whom, that, which,* and *whose:*

> **6.19** She reprimanded the waiter [*who* spilled the soup].
>
> **6.20** Judy Reynolds is a woman [*whom* we respect greatly].
>
> **6.21** The car [*that* I bought] is almost new.
>
> **6.22** The movie [*which* you saw] was a rerun.
>
> **6.23** I saw the man [*whose* house was burglarized].

Like interrogative pronouns, relatives occur at the beginning of the clause to which they belong, and they may stand for any noun phrase, whether it is a subject, a direct object, an object of a preposition, or any other function:

6.24a *The glass* broke. (subject)

   b *that* broke

   c The glass [that broke] belonged to my grandmother.

6.25a We bought *the milk*. (direct object)

   b *that* we bought

   c The milk [that we bought] tasted peculiar.

6.26a She showed *the man* the letter. (indirect object)

   b *whom* she showed the letter

   c The man [whom she showed the letter] stole it.

6.27a You are referring to *the short story*. (object of a preposition)

   b to *which* you are referring

   c The short story [to which you are referring] was written by Faulkner.

6.28a They called him *a name*. (objective complement)

   b *that* they called him

   c The name [that they called him] was degrading.

In each sentence the relative pronoun occurs at the beginning of the clause and not at the usual place for a direct object, an objective complement, or the like.

Although relative pronouns may look somewhat like interrogatives, this similarity is largely confined to their being positioned at the beginning. For the interrogatives, we do not know what is being referred to, but for the relatives we do know the referent. Furthermore, interrogative pronouns introduce questions, but relative pronouns do not. Instead of eliciting information, relative pronouns introduce clauses that modify nouns.

Who and *whom* are used to refer only to humans, *which* to nonhumans, and *that* to either.

6.29a I picked up the boy [*who* fell from the roof].

   b *I picked up the boy [*which* fell from the roof].

   c I picked up the boy [*that* fell from the roof].

> **6.30a** *I picked up the rock [*who* fell from the roof].
>   **b**   I picked up the rock [*which* fell from the roof].
>   **c**   I picked up the rock [*that* fell from the roof].

Many people feel more comfortable using *whose* to refer to humans than to nonhumans:

> **6.31**   I hit the man [*whose* language disgusted me].
> **6.32**   ?I sold the chair [*whose* color disgusted me].

However, there is no satisfactory substitute for nonhumans, and a structure such as the following is awkward:

> **6.33**   I sold the chair [the color of which disgusted me].

To avoid sentences like **6.33**, many people accept the use of *whose* for nonhumans.

When the relative pronoun is the object of a preposition, the preposition may be found either at the beginning of the clause or at the end:

> **6.34a**   The people [*about* whom we were talking] left.
>   **b**   The people [whom we were talking *about*] left.

The **b** version with the preposition at the end of the clause is less formal than the **a** version. For such sentences some people prefer to use the informal *who* to maintain a consistent style:

> **6.34c**   The people [who we were talking about] left.

With objects of prepositions there are restrictions on the use of the pronoun *that:*

> **6.34d**   The people [*that* we were talking about] left.
>   **e**   *The people [about *that* we were talking] left.

Whereas *that* is possible when the preposition comes at the end of the clause, it is not allowed when the preposition precedes it.

At times the relative pronoun is understood but does not actually occur:

6.35a   The picture [that you drew] wasn't very good.

   b   The picture [you drew] wasn't very good.

6.36a   The people [whom we showed the letter] laughed.

   b   The people [we showed the letter] laughed.

6.37a   I met the woman [whom you were pointing to].

   b   I met the woman [you were pointing to].

Yet there are restrictions:

6.37c   *I met the woman [to you were pointing].

   d   I met the woman [to whom you were pointing].

When a preposition precedes a relative pronoun, it may not be omitted. Also relative pronouns functioning as subjects must be present:

6.38a   I despise people [who laugh at me].

   b   *I despise people [laugh at me].

Only object pronouns may be omitted—direct objects, indirect objects, objective complements, and objects of prepositions. Relative pronouns that are objects of prepositions may be omitted only if the prepositions do not precede them.

   Relative clauses may be introduced by **relative adverbs** as well as relative pronouns:

6.39a   The town [in *which* I was born] is small. (pronoun)

   b   The town [*where* I was born] is small. (adverb)

6.40a   The time [at *which* we could sell] has passed. (pronoun)

   b   The time [*when* we could sell] has passed. (adverb)

6.41a   That is the reason [for *which* she left]. (pronoun)

   b   That is the reason [*why* she left]. (adverb)

The **a** versions contain relative pronouns used as objects of prepositions. In the **b** sentences, however, the entire prepositional phrases have been replaced by the relative adverbs *where, when,* and *why*. Notice that the dependent clauses in the **b** sentences are still relative clauses because they modify the nouns *town, time,* and *reason*. Do not mistake them for adverb clauses just because they begin with adverbs.

A relative clause may modify a noun or pronoun within another dependent clause:

> **6.42a** We were amused by the comments [that were made by the student].
>
> **b** We were amused by the comments [that were made by the student [who was sitting by the door]].

Since a clause consists of subject, verb, object or complement, and all modifiers of these elements, the first relative clause is *that were made by the student who was sitting by the door*. Within it is embedded the clause *who was sitting by the door*, modifying the object of the preposition *student*. Such embedding is not limited to one clause:

> **6.42c** We were amused by the comments [that were made by the student [who was sitting by the door [that opened into the laboratory]]].

We may keep adding clauses as long as we have something worthwhile to say and are not confusing or irritating our readers.

PARTICIPIAL PHRASES

For economy we often reduce relative clauses to more compact structures known as **participial phrases;** that is, instead of using full relative clauses like the **a** versions below, we use the **b** versions:

> **6.43a** The snow [that is falling today] isn't sticking.
>
> **b** The snow [falling today] isn't sticking.
>
> **6.44a** I startled the man [who is sitting by the window].
>
> **b** I startled the man [sitting by the window].
>
> **6.45a** We ran to the girl [who was motioning to us].
>
> **b** We ran to the girl [motioning to us].

Participial phrases can be paraphrased with relative clauses that contain a form of *be*. They do not contain relative pronouns, nor do they show tense.

We can illustrate the absence of tense with the following sentences:

> **6.46a** The salesman [who was knocking at the door] irritated me.
>
> **b** The salesman [knocking at the door] irritated me.
>
> **6.47a** The salesman [who is knocking at the door] irritated me.
>
> **b** The salesman [knocking at the door] irritated me.

The acts of knocking and irritating may or may not have occurred at the same time, and they are not necessarily related. Whether the knocking occurred prior to the act of speaking or simultaneously with it, it still appears as *knocking at the door*. This distinction is found in the full clause in the tense of *be: was* or *is*. There is no such indication for the participle.

Participles ending in *-ing* are traditionally known as **present participles**, as opposed to **past participles** such as those in the **b** sentences below:

> **6.48a** The woman [who was pushed down the stairs] was not hurt.
>
> **b** The woman [pushed down the stairs] was not hurt.
>
> **6.49a** We pitied the man [who was mauled by the lion].
>
> **b** We pitied the man [mauled by the lion].
>
> **6.50a** The letter [that was written by Carolyn] was funny.
>
> **b** The letter [written by Carolyn] was funny.

As comparison of the **a** and **b** versions shows, past participial phrases can be paraphrased with passive relative clauses containing *be*. As the name suggests, past participial phrases begin with past participles, the same form that follows the auxiliary *have* and the passive *be:*

> **6.51** We have *chosen* the winner.
>
> **6.52** The winner was *chosen* by us.
>
> **6.53** The man *chosen* by us will not fail.

Like present participial phrases, they do not show tense:

> **6.54a** The people [who are insulted by your remarks] will be unfriendly.

b   The people [insulted by your remarks] will be unfriendly.

6.55a   The people [who were insulted by your remarks] will be unfriendly.

b   The people [insulted by your remarks] will be unfriendly.

Whereas relative clauses show tense, participial phrases do not.

The terms *present participle* and *past participle* are unfortunate because they suggest present and past tense. Both participles may denote action taking place at the same time as another act in the sentence or at the time of the utterance. More accurate names would be *active* and *passive participles* because they correspond to active and passive relative clauses, respectively. A few examples will illustrate:

6.56a   The man [who is kicking the horse] will suffer.

b   The man [kicking the horse] will suffer.

c   The man [who was kicked by the horse] will suffer.

d   The man [kicked by the horse] will suffer.

6.57a   The postman [who was biting the dog] will get rabies.

b   The postman [biting the dog] will get rabies.

c   The postman [who is bitten by the dog] will get rabies.

d   The postman [bitten by the dog] will get rabies.

The **a** and **b** sentences identify the man or postman by an action that he performed; in the **c** and **d** sentences the action happened to him. The two kinds of participles show active and passive voice, not present and past time. In spite of these problems, the names *present* and *past participle* are so widely used that we will continue to use them, noting that they do not refer to tense.

Although participles do not express tense, they do tell whether the action is in progress or completed. The present participle is always progressive, as we see when we paraphrase it with a verb in a relative clause:

6.58a   The burglar [who is robbing your house] will be disappointed.

b   The burglar [robbing your house] will be disappointed.

Sentences **6.58a** and **6.58b** both contain active phrases or clauses. There is also a passive progressive. Like any other passive, it is formed with the auxiliary *be* followed by the past participle:

6.59a The house [that is being robbed by a burglar] belongs to the Lambs.

   b The house [being robbed by a burglar] belongs to the Lambs.

In addition, there are perfect participles, formed with the auxiliary *have;* as we saw in Chapter 3, the auxiliary *have* is followed by a past participle:

6.60a My sister, [who has bought a new car], is now impecunious.

   b My sister, [having bought a new car], is now impecunious.

And there is a perfect passive participle:

6.61a The woman [who had been invited to the reception] laughed with embarrassment.

   b The woman, [having been invited to the reception], laughed with embarrassment.

In the preceding sentence, we see the auxiliary *have* followed by the past participle *been* and the passive *be* followed by the past participle *invited*. Theoretically it is possible to have a final combination of auxiliaries with a participle, *have*, and the progressive *be:*

6.62a Those people [who have been sneering at me all night] finally left.

   b Those people, [having been sneering at me all night], finally left.

As the forced nature of this example shows, this structure is rarely found.

   Like verbs, participles may take complements and adverbial modifiers:

Direct Object

6.63a   The person [who is hitting *me*] had better stop.

b   The person [hitting *me*] had better stop.

Predicate Adjective

6.64a   The girl [who was looking unhappy] left the room.

b   The girl [looking *unhappy*] left the room.

Objective Complement

6.65a   Anyone [who is calling me *stupid*] will get hit.

b   Anyone [calling me *stupid*] will get hit.

Adverbial Modifier

6.66a   The people [who were talking *in the hallway*] disturbed me.

b   The people [talking *in the hallway*] disturbed me.

Furthermore, as we saw with past participles, they may be passive. These similarities between participles and verbs are not surprising if we think of participial phrases as reduced relative clauses. With such an interpretation, they *are* verbs that have had tense removed. Also, it is not the participle alone that modifies a noun but the entire participial phrase, just as it is the entire relative clause that modifies, not just the verb in it.

When a participle is intransitive and has no modifiers, it often occurs before the noun, the same as an adjective:

6.67a   A dog [that is snarling] is dangerous.

b   A [snarling] dog is dangerous.

6.68a   We hid the letter [that we opened].

b   We hid the [opened] letter.

Unlike adjectives, some participles may follow the noun:

6.69a   A *smiling* beggar is suspicious.

b   A beggar *smiling* is suspicious.

6.70a   A *richly dressed* beggar is suspicious.

b   A beggar *richly dressed* is suspicious.

6.71a   A *handsome* beggar is suspicious.

 b   *A beggar *handsome* is suspicious.

Whereas **6.71b** might be acceptable in poetry, it is impossible in prose.

ADVERBIALS

It is traditionally assumed that only adjectives can modify nouns, but adverbials of place often do so as well. For example, we can readily find examples like the **b** versions below:

6.72a   The people [who are outside] are noisy.

 b   The people [outside] are noisy.

6.73a   The books [that are there] are valuable.

 b   The books [there] are valuable.

6.74a   I was talking to the man [who was ahead].

 b   I was talking to the man [ahead].

Prepositional phrases may also modify nouns:

6.75a   The coat [that is on the chair] is wet.

 b   The coat [on the chair] is wet.

6.76a   The people [who were between the cars] frightened me.

 b   The people [between the cars] frightened me.

Note that these structures are clearly adverbials of place when the full relative clause is given, as in the **a** versions. If we consider the **b** versions as reduced relative clauses, it no longer seems strange that adverbials of place appear to modify nouns.

RESTRICTIVE AND NONRESTRICTIVE MODIFIERS

The noun modifiers that we have examined so far serve the function of restricting the class of objects under discussion, either to a subclass or to a unique individual. In the following sentence, for example, the relative clause indicates which boy is intended:

6.77   I threw the sandwich to the boy [who stood behind Al].

Some nouns are shown to be unique by other means, such as the following:

6.78   I threw the sandwich to Raul, [who stood behind Al].

Here the proper noun identifies the person, and the relative clause gives added information. In fact, sentence **6.78** could almost be paraphrased with a compound sentence:

6.79   I threw the sandwich to Raul, and he stood behind Al.

A compound sentence such as this loses the notion of subordination found in **6.78**; it is, therefore, not a real paraphrase. We call a modifier that does not serve the function of restricting the class of objects named a **nonrestrictive modifier;** one that restricts is called a **restrictive modifier**.

Here are some additional examples of restrictive and nonrestrictive modifiers:

6.80a   We discussed the movie [that we had seen four times].

b   We discussed *Gone With the Wind*, [which we had seen four times].

6.81a   The city [that I visited last week] has hot summers.

b   Chicago, [which I visited last week], has hot summers.

6.82a   She wrote a paper on the planet [that she had been observing through a telescope].

b   She wrote a paper on Mars, [which she had been observing through a telescope].

6.83a   The actress [whom I admire so much] is in a new play.

b   Lucy Conlin, [whom I admire so much], is in a new play.

In the **b** sentences the proper noun is already identified; the nonrestrictive clause merely supplies added information. In the **a** ver-

sions, however, we do not know which movie, city, planet, or actress is intended without the restrictive clause.

At times there are several people or objects with the same
name, making the noun common. In such instances the article *the*
and a restrictive clause are found:

> **6.84** The Helen Adams [to whom I referred] is not asso-
> ciated with this firm.
>
> **6.85** Which of the Springfields [that are in the Midwest]
> do you mean?
>
> **6.86** *The Secret Agent* [that I recommended to you] is the
> one by Joseph Conrad.

In each of these sentences, the relative clause is restrictive.

At other times a possessive or adjective specifies the noun,
and the relative clause is nonrestrictive. In the **a** versions below,
the clause is restrictive; in the **b** versions, nonrestrictive:

> **6.87a** I was talking to a mother [who detests poems about
> motherhood].
>
> **b** I was talking to Sheila's mother, [who detests
> poems about motherhood].
>
> **6.88a** Her daughter [who lives in Columbus] is an or-
> nithologist.
>
> **b** Her youngest daughter, [who lives in Columbus], is
> an ornithologist.
>
> **6.89a** We were discussing his grandmother [who is skiing
> in the Alps].
>
> **b** We were discussing his maternal grandmother,
> [who is skiing in the Alps].

Once we label the noun as *Sheila's mother, her youngest daughter,* or
his maternal grandmother, we know which one is meant.

Shared knowledge may be enough to restrict a noun. For
example, if the speaker can assume that the listener knows he has
only one brother, he may say the following:

> **6.90** My brother, [who went to Greece last summer],
> brought back some interesting post cards.

The designation *my brother* is enough to indicate which one is
meant. Similarly, if we know that Bob has only one car, *Bob's car* is

enough to specify the object we are discussing, and any accompanying relative clause will be nonrestrictive. If we are speaking of our solar system, *the sun* indicates the source of light that is meant; similarly, we may refer to *the moon* to indicate the heavenly body that circles the earth.

When we examine relative clauses with indefinite pronouns or adjectives, we discover a peculiar relationship. Notice the difference in meaning between the **a** sentences with the restrictive clauses and the **b** sentences without them:

> **6.91a**   Anyone [who remembers these directions] can find my house easily.
>
> **b**   Anyone can find my house easily.
>
> **6.92a**   All teachers [who turn their grades in on time] will be rewarded.
>
> **b**   All teachers will be rewarded.

In sentences such as these, the clauses still function to limit the class (*ones, teachers*). In **6.92a**, for example, of all the teachers in existence, it is only those who turn their grades in on time who will be rewarded. However, the **b** sentences are not just less specific versions of the **a** sentences; they mean something different. The indefinite word—*any, all, each, every*—is closely tied to the relative clause, and if we omit one we must omit the other as well. Unfortunately, too much emphasis on sentences like **6.91** and **6.92** led some earlier grammarians to state that a restrictive clause is essential to the meaning of the sentence, whereas a nonrestrictive clause is not. Such a statement is absurd; unless the nonrestrictive modifier is redundant, it is as essential to "meaning" as the restrictive modifier is. The two differ in that one serves a limiting function and the other does not.

The semantic differences between restrictive and nonrestrictive clauses are matched with those of intonation and choice of relative pronoun. Nonrestrictive clauses are set off by pauses in speech and by commas in writing:

> **6.93a**   The Dean, [who listens to all grade complaints], is out of town this week.

If the school has only one dean or if the context makes it clear which one is meant (e.g., the conversation takes place in a certain dean's office), the relative clause is nonrestrictive. On the other hand, if the clause is used to indicate a particular dean, it is restrictive:

6.93b   The dean [who listens to all grade complaints] is out of town this week.

Comma intonation is found with the nonrestrictive clause but not with the restrictive.

For restrictive clauses the full range of relative pronouns may be selected: *who, whom, which, whose, that.* For nonrestrictives, *that* is not permitted.

6.94a   She scolded the child [*that* was playing in the mud].

   b   *She scolded Barry, [*that* was playing in the mud].

Nonrestrictive clauses permit only *who/whom* for humans, *which* for nonhumans, and *whose* for possessives.

Another difference between the two kinds of clauses can be seen in the deletability of the relative pronoun. Object relatives may be deleted in restrictive clauses, but they must be retained in nonrestrictives:

6.95a   The city [we visited last spring] was interesting.

   b   *Atlanta, [we visited last spring], was interesting.

   c   Atlanta, [which we visited last spring], was interesting.

Restrictive and nonrestrictive clauses differ not only in meaning, but also in form.

What we have said about clauses is also largely true of participial phrases:

6.96a   My brother [who was standing by the curb] was almost hit by a car.

   b   My brother [standing by the curb] was almost hit by a car.

6.97a   My youngest brother, [who was standing by the curb], was almost hit by a car.

   b   My youngest brother, [standing by the curb], was almost hit by a car.

In **6.96**, both the relative clause and the participial phrase identify which brother is meant, even though his position is unquestionably important. In **6.97**, however, the word *youngest* identifies the brother; the clause or phrase is important only for the information it contains, not for identifying the noun.

Unlike clauses, nonrestrictive participial phrases may occur at various places in the sentence, not just directly after the nouns they modify. For example, any of these versions is possible:

6.98a Brenda, [leaning out the window], called loudly.

   b [Leaning out the window], Brenda called loudly.

   c Brenda called loudly, [leaning out the window].

Such freedom does not exist with clauses:

6.99a Brenda, [who was leaning out the window], called loudly.

   b *[Who was leaning out the window], Brenda called loudly.

   c *Brenda called loudly, [who was leaning out the window].

In fact, the position of nonrestrictive participial phrases at the beginning or the end of the sentence is more usual for many writers than that directly after the noun.

We may paraphrase sentences with nonrestrictive participial phrases as compound sentences, as we did nonrestrictive clauses:

6.100a Laughing obstreperously, Harry declined the invitation.

   b Harry was laughing obstreperously, and he declined the invitation.

They may also be paraphrased in most cases with adverbial clauses:

6.100c While he was laughing obstreperously, Harry declined the invitation.

Or with the following structure:

6.100d While laughing obstreperously, Harry declined the invitation.

Some grammarians call *while laughing obstreperously* an **elliptical clause** because it seems to have *he was* omitted. However, this is inconsistent unless we are prepared to call all participial phrases elliptical clauses, because they can all be looked upon as reduced relative clauses.

EXERCISES

A. Replace the complex noun phrases in the following sentences with proper nouns.

> **example:**   The man who opened the door insulted everyone.
> *Harry* insulted everyone.

1. Did you thank the taxi driver who found your gloves?
2. Someone sent my friend who lives in Tucson a magazine subscription.
3. I stayed for a month in that city on the Seine.
4. The man climbing that mountain will probably fall.
5. Did you see the movie that everyone is raving about?

B. Enclose each relative clause in brackets and draw an arrow to the noun it modifies. Then paraphrase the clause with a complete sentence and tell how the relative pronoun functions.

> **example:**   I finally killed the fly [that had been bothering me].
> Paraphrase: The fly had been bothering me.
> *That* functions as subject.

1. We found a door that was unlocked.
2. Her mother considers her a person whom everyone should admire.
3. We handed it to the worker who stood by the door.
4. Did you write the article that we were talking about?
5. Everyone is distressed by the kind of person that he has become.
6. They gave the movie which we saw a bad review.
7. The name that they called him was ridiculous.
8. The person to whom you should write is the manager.
9. She is a bore whom no one likes.
10. Anyone who laughs at me will be sorry.

C. Rewrite the following pairs of sentences as single sentences in which the second one is a relative clause embedded within the first:

example: **a** The sweater is old.
   b I gave her the sweater.
   The sweater that I gave her is old.

1a. I wrote a poem.
  b. Everyone is laughing at my poem.
2a. The key belongs to me.
  b. You found the key.
3a. Someone threw a rock at the car.
  b. The car raced down the street.
4a. I bought a new hat.
  b. I will not wear the new hat until next summer.
5a. The river is now hazardous.
  b. We used to swim in the river.
6a. The teacher began screaming.
  b. We drove the teacher crazy.
7a. She opened the door for the man.
  b. The man was carrying a package.
8a. The people seemed appreciative.
  b. We gave the tickets to the people.
9a. Harold sneered at the poem.
  b. I had written the poem.
10a. The house was insured.
  b. The house burned.

D. Explain why some of the following sentences are un-grammatical. Note: Some are correct.

  1. The girl which laughed made a fool of herself.
  2. Did you thank the man that gave you the quarter?
  3. Did you see the movie which I recommended?
  4. I don't like dogs who bark at me.
  5. The dog who greeted us at the door asked us to be seated.
  6. The book we were looking at has disappeared.
  7. The tree to which we walked was only a mile from the house.
  8. Did you see the man pushed you?
  9. The boy to I gave the dollar was grateful.
  10. The child the teacher scolded cried.

E. How many tests can you use to show that the italicized group of words in each of these sentences is or is not a noun phrase?

1. *Those crimson sheets that you bought for your bed* shocked Martha.

2. Harvey must have seen *the young man in the tuxedo last evening*.

F. Rewrite each of the following sentences, changing the relative clauses to participial or prepositional phrases. Then tell what kind of phrase each one is: present participial, past participial, or prepositional.

1. The boorish man who is sleeping on his back has begun to snore.

2. Did you cook the rooster that was hit by the truck?

3. He sent it to the student who is waiting outside.

4. Do those socks that are in the dryer belong to you?

5. The ham that was baked in the microwave oven was delicious.

6. Someone who was sitting in the front row was making rude noises.

7. He likes none of the people who are at work.

8. I handed the person who was in front of me a coupon.

9. Is she the woman who was shoved in front of a car?

10. The student who is writing his answers in red ink is in for a surprise.

G. Give the structure (relative clause, prepositional phrase, noun phrase, etc.) of each italicized group of words and tell how it functions (direct object, adverbial of time, modifier of *room*, etc.).

example: a   We gave *the child in the school yard* a ball.
                    noun phrase—indirect object
               b   The man *by the tree* is a nuisance.
                    prepositional phrase—modifies *man*

1. Harriet mailed the letter to her cousin *in Philadelphia*.

2. The plane will depart *at midnight*.

3. She has become *the most notorious woman in Canada*.

4. Those people *shivering by the fence* look cold.

5. The judges awarded the poem *submitted by Jack* first prize.

6. The program has been canceled because of a *wretched* mix up.
7. His *broken* arm prevented him from playing.
8. The trustees will appoint him *head librarian for the campus*.
9. Never has there been *a more egotistical person* than you.
10. *At the next corner* will you let me out?
11. *Who on earth* could it be?
12. He was in *the sitting room*.
13. I will help anyone *who asks for my assistance*.
14. The clouds *above* look threatening.
15. Is that your *leather* skirt?
16. Everywhere *we go* we see Judy.
17. Did you leave your shoes *outside?*
18. I could hardly stay on that *bucking* horse.
19. The *upstairs* offices are noisy.
20. I baked the cookies *you like so much*.

H. Write original sentences following the patterns given below:

1. Subject + Relative Clause–Verb–Predicate Noun
2. Time–Subject–Verb–Direct Object + Present Participial Phrase
3. Subject–Verb–Indirect Object + Prepositional Phrase–Direct Object
4. Subject + Past Participial Phrase–Verb–Predicate Adjective
5. Subject + Present Participial Phrase–Verb–Direct Object–Manner

I. The following passages have been written so that most noun modifiers appear in independent clauses. Revise them so that the sentences are less choppy and less important ideas are subordinated.

1. The lady laughed again. She was dark. They both relapsed upon the view. They were contemplating it in silence, and there was a sort of serenity. This serenity was diffused, and it might have been borrowed from the spring effulgence of the Roman skies.

2. The waiting room was not an inviting place. It was lit by the oil lamps, and they flared a red light over the benches. The red light was dull, and the benches were dingy.

3. But the Prince Prospero was happy and dauntless and sagacious. When his dominions were half depopulated, he summoned to his presence a thousand friends from among the knights and ladies of his court. These friends were hale and light-hearted. With them he retired to the seclusion of one of his abbeys. The seclusion was deep, and the abbey was castellated.

4. Hester Prynne went, one day, to the mansion of Governor Bellingham, with a pair of gloves. She had fringed and embroidered the gloves to his order, and they were to be worn on some great occasion of state.

5. On the other side he looked down into a mountain glen. It was deep, wild, lonely, and shagged. The bottom was filled with fragments from the cliffs. The cliffs were impending. The bottom was scarcely lighted by the rays of the sun. The rays were reflected, and the sun was setting.

chapter 7 ══════════════

Phrases and Clauses as Noun Phrases

The simplest kind of sentence is one with SVO order and a minimum number of words for each function:

7.1 My cousin saw a woman there.

We can easily recognize the subject, verb, direct object, and adverbial. With the addition of auxiliaries, we may expand the verb:

7.2 My cousin *must have seen* a woman there.

Or instead of a single-word adverbial, we may use a prepositional phrase:

7.3 My cousin must have seen a woman *at the carnival.*

Nouns may be modified by various structures, making them complex:

7.4 *My young cousin who is visiting me this week* must have seen a woman at the carnival.

7.5 My young cousin who is visiting me this week must have seen *a woman condemning smoking* at the carnival.

7.6 My young cousin who is visiting me this week must have seen a woman condemning smoking at *the carnival in the next county*.

Regardless of how far we expand each element, we still have the same basic structure as we did for **7.1**: subject, verb, direct object, adverbial of place.

A noun modifier may be a single word, such as an article, a possessive, a demonstrative, or an adjective, in which case it usually precedes the noun; or it may be a participial phrase or a relative clause, following the noun. There are various structures that modify nouns, but they all have the same function. If they are restrictive, their function is different from that of nonrestrictive modifiers.

NOUN CLAUSES

Instead of using a noun with modifiers to function as a subject, direct object, object of a preposition, and the like, we may use a **noun clause:**

7.7 Hiram believes [that he is right].

In this sentence the entire structure *that he is right* functions as the direct object of *believes*, as we can see if we substitute the pronoun *it* for the structure:

7.8 Hiram believes *it*.

The noun clause *that he is right* consists of the complete sentence *He is right*, to which the **conjunction** *that* has been attached. Unlike the relative pronoun *that*, the conjunction does not function as a subject, direct object, or the like.

Noun clauses may function in most of the ways that nouns do:

Subject

7.9a *This fact* is a shame.

  b [That you are ugly] is a shame.

Predicate Noun

7.10a The problem is *this*.

   b The problem is [that I've caught my hand in a jar].

Direct Object

7.11a She knows *the answer*.

   b She knows [that you are the guilty one].

Except when the clause begins the sentence, *that* may be omitted:

7.12a The answer was [that I was sick of her].

   b The answer was [I was sick of her].

7.13a She said [that she was lucky].

   b She said [she was lucky].

At the beginning of the sentence, *that* may not be omitted:

7.14a [That you will win the medal] seems unlikely.

   b *[You will win the medal] seems unlikely.

The reason for this restriction is that without *that* we have no way to recognize the structure as a noun clause. Therefore, we read *You will win the medal* as the main clause until we reach the verb *seems*, when we realize that something is wrong and go back. To avoid this kind of confusion, we always retain *that* when the clause comes at the beginning.

Subject noun clauses are often **extraposed** to the end of the sentence and their slot is filled with the **expletive** *it*. For example, we may have a sentence with a noun clause subject such as this:

7.15a [That you are so indifferent] bothers me.

We may move the noun clause to the end:

7.15b bothers me [that you are so indifferent].

Then, to fill the subject position, we add *it*, a word with no lexical meaning:

7.15c *It* bothers me [that you are so indifferent].

We call *that you are so indifferent* the subject both in **7.15a** and **7.15c**. Extraposed subjects are also known as **delayed subjects**.

Here are some additional examples of extraposed subject noun clauses:

7.16a [That he will be on time] seems doubtful.

 b *It* seems doubtful [that he will be on time].

7.17a [That you got caught in traffic] amused me.

 b *It* amused me [that you got caught in traffic].

In the **b** versions *that* may be omitted, because the noun clauses no longer come at the beginning of the sentence.

Although both the **a** and **b** versions of **7.16** and **7.17** are possible, those without extraposition seem somewhat formal. We extrapose subject noun clauses more often than we leave them in their basic position. At times, such as when the verb has nothing after it, extraposition is obligatory:

7.18a *[That they are divorced] happens.

 b *It* happens [that they are divorced].

7.19a *[That he is in a bad mood] appears.

 b *It* appears [that he is in a bad mood].

The **a** versions are not possible English sentences, as the asterisk indicates.

Noun clauses functioning as direct objects may be extraposed in the same manner as those acting as subjects:

7.20a We think [that you will be sued] unlikely.

 b We think *it* unlikely [that you will be sued].

When a noun clause direct object has an objective complement, extraposition is almost always performed. Extraposed objects are also known as **delayed objects**.

Some noun clauses function as **appositives**. Let us first review this function with single nouns:

7.21 My friend *Jane* opened the package.

7.22 He went back to his home town, *Longview*.

In each instance, the appositive renames the noun preceding it. If the appositive is restrictive, as it is in **7.21**, it gives a more precise name; that is, we assume that the speaker has more than one friend. *Jane* serves the function of limiting the class as an adjective would (e.g., *my oldest friend*). When the appositive is nonrestrictive, as in **7.22**, it does not restrict the noun it follows but rather gives more specific information about it. As the examples indicate, nonrestrictive appositives are set off with commas, but those that are restrictive are not. They follow the same principles as other restrictive and nonrestrictive elements, such as relative clauses.

Now let us look at noun clauses that function as appositives:

7.23   The assumption [that I will pay the bill] is faulty.

7.24   We considered the suggestion [that no one should go].

7.25   The fact [that we are learning a great deal] is obvious.

In each instance the noun clause gives a more specific statement of what the assumption, suggestion, or fact is. These are restrictive appositives.

Appositive noun clauses look a great deal like relative clauses, especially as both may begin with the word *that*. However, they can easily be shown to be quite different. First of all, they have a different semantic relationship to the noun they follow:

7.26   The suggestion [that he made] amused me.

7.27   The suggestion [that he should go] amused me.

In **7.26**, *that he made* is a relative clause. We do not know what the suggestion is but merely which one is being mentioned. In **7.27**, however, *that he should go* is an appositive, telling us specifically what the suggestion is.

As we look more closely at the two sentences, we see further differences. *That* in **7.26** is a relative pronoun, functioning as the object of *made*. Furthermore, it means *the suggestion*. As a relative pronoun, it can be replaced by *which:*

7.28   The suggestion [*which* he made] amused me.

In **7.27**, however, *that* has no lexical meaning; it merely serves to introduce the noun clause. And it does not have a syntactic function such as subject or object. It would be impossible to substitute *which* for it:

7.29 *The suggestion [*which* he should go] amused me.

Noun clauses beginning with *that* may look like relative clauses, but upon closer inspection we can see that they are different.

There is another structure that is even more difficult to classify. Grammarians in the past have not agreed on whether to call it a noun clause or a relative clause:

7.30 [What you said] bothered me.

7.31 I know [who brought the present].

7.32 She will give it to [whoever asks for it].

Because the structure can be replaced by a pronoun, we shall call it a noun clause, even though the meaning seems closer to that of a relative clause.

As with noun clauses beginning with *that*, those with WH words may function in most ways that nouns and pronouns do:

Subject

7.33 [Whatever you give him] will make him happy.

Direct Object

7.34 Betty believed [what you said].

Indirect Object

7.35 She will send [whoever answers the question] a prize.

Predicate Noun

7.36 That is not [what I said].

Objective Complement

7.37 I will call you [whatever I please].

Object of a Preposition

7.38 She will sit beside [whom she chooses].

These noun clauses are like relative clauses and questions in that they begin with a WH word that has been moved from its basic position in the sentence. We can illustrate this positioning by using the pronouns *something* and *someone* in the **a** versions below, where they are in their basic position; in the **b** versions they have been moved to the beginning and replaced with WH words:

7.39a We read *something*.
  b *what* we read
7.40a *Someone* asks the first question.
  b *whoever* asks the first question
7.41a She gave *someone* the ticket.
  b *whom* she gave the ticket

Like relative clauses, noun clauses can be paraphrased with complete sentences, and the WH words have specific functions such as subject or direct object within that sentence.

For those people who never use *whom*, there is no problem with which pronoun to use to represent humans; for those who follow the conventional practice of using *who* for subjects and predicate nouns and *whom* for all kinds of objects, it is essential to recognize how the pronoun is used within the noun clause. In the following sentence, for example, *who* is the subject of *sent:*

7.42 We know [*who* sent the money].

The entire noun clause is the object of *know*, as we can see if we replace it with a pronoun:

7.43 We know *that*.

If we substitute a noun for the pronoun *who*, converting the noun clause into a sentence, we readily see that it is the subject:

7.44a *who* sent the money
  b *Frank* sent the money.

When objects of prepositions are involved, either in the main or the noun clause, special care needs to be given to the structure:

7.45a We talked about [*who* would grade the papers].

   b We talked about *something*.

   c *Professor Horne* would grade the papers.

Whereas there may be some confusion as to what the object of *about* is in **7.45a**, if we substitute the pronoun *something* for the noun clause, as in **7.45b**, we see that the entire clause is the object of the preposition. Furthermore, if we replace *who* with a noun, as in **7.45c**, we see that it is the subject of *would grade*. Here is another example:

   7.46a We know [about *whom* you are writing].

      b We know *something*.

      c You are writing about *Hans Hellmut Kirst*.

As we can see from the **b** and **c** versions, *about* is part of the noun clause, and the pronoun *whom* is its object.

    It is possible to have more than one noun clause in a sentence, just as it is possible to have more than one relative clause. One way to do this is to let both subject and predicate noun be clauses:

   7.47 [What I am trying to say] is [that this will not do].

Or we may add a noun clause within another one. For example, we may start with:

   7.48a Grace thinks [that John believes something].

Instead of *something*, we may use a noun clause:

   7.48b Grace thinks [that John believes [she told everyone something]].

Again, we may replace *something* with a noun clause:

   7.48c Grace thinks [that John believes [she told everyone [that he thinks something]]].

Now that we have made our point, let us cut the sentence off with one more addition:

   7.48d Grace thinks [that John believes [she told everyone [that he thinks [that he can fly]]]].

Such lengthy expansions become awkward and stylistically unpalatable, but theoretically we can continue them without limit.

When sentences containing noun clauses are turned into questions, the syntactic functions of all elements may not be immediately clear. For example, we may have a sentence such as this:

7.49a He thinks [Albert will wash the car].

We can analyze the sentence without pausing. If we convert this into a yes–no question, we derive the following:

7.49b Does he think [Albert will wash the car]?

Still there is no difficulty. However, if we turn this into a WH question, using an interrogative pronoun to replace *Albert*, we complicate the sentence:

7.49c *Who* does he think [will wash the car]?

The subject of the noun clause has been moved to the beginning of the entire sentence. This arrangement plus the inverted word order *does he think* may make the function of *who* difficult for some people to determine. Here are some additional examples, in which related sentences are given without inversion:

7.50a *Whom* did you say you saw?
   b You said [you saw *Herman*].
7.51a *Who* will she assume opened the bottle?
   b She will assume [*I* opened the bottle].
7.52a To *whom* do they believe we sent the money?
   b They believe [we sent the money to *Virginia*].

The paraphrases clearly show how the interrogative pronouns function.

GERUND PHRASES

As we have seen, several different structures may function as subject, direct object, and the like:

Noun by Itself

7.53   *Sarah* startled everyone.

Noun with Modifiers

7.54   *The woman who was brushing her teeth in the restaurant* startled everyone.

Noun Clause with a WH Word

7.55   *What you did* startled everyone.

Noun Clause with *that*

7.56   It startled everyone *that you knew the answer*.

Pronoun

7.57   *She* startled everyone.

We can now add another structure, the **gerund phrase:**

7.58   [Ann's opening the window] startled everyone.

A gerund phrase is formed from a sentence, as we can see by comparing the following versions:

7.59a   Ann opened the window.
   b   Ann's opening the window.

In both the sentence **a** and the gerund phrase **b**, *Ann* is the agent that performed the act of opening, and *the window* is the object that was affected by the action. The same subject-verb-object relationship is apparent in both. They differ in form in that the sentence contains tense, which is missing in the gerund phrase; for the latter, the subject is a possessive (*Ann's*), and the verb ends in *-ing* (*opening*).

A gerund phrase may function in many of the ways that a pronoun or other noun phrase does:

Subject

7.60a *It* amused me.

    b [Your losing your false teeth] amused me.

Direct Object

7.61a We enjoyed *it*.

    b We enjoyed [Carl's telling us about his trip].

Predicate Noun

7.62a Our most boring moment was *that*.

    b Our most boring moment was [his reciting that poem].

Object of a Preposition

7.63a We talked about *it*.

    b We talked about [your leaving so early].

Indirect Object

7.64a We gave *it* no attention.

    b We gave [your boasting] no attention.

Since gerund phrases are derived from sentences, it is not surprising that they contain the same elements that sentences do. Here are a few examples:

Subject–Verb–Indirect Object–Direct Object

7.65a Paula handed Tom the script.

    b Paula's handing Tom the script

Subject–Verb–Direct Object–Objective Complement

7.66a William left her alone.

    b William's leaving her alone

Subject–Verb–Predicate Adjective

7.67a   She looked frightened.

   b   her looking frightened

Subject–Verb–Adverbial of Time

7.68a   He yelled during the lunch break.

   b   his yelling during the lunch break

Almost any sentence can be converted into a gerund phrase.

Whenever the subject of a gerund phrase names the same person or object that is mentioned in the main clause, it is deleted; that is, we have the **a** version below but not the **b:**

7.69a   Lois regretted [Karen's having seen the mess].

   b   *Lois regretted [Lois' having seen the mess].

If we substitute a pronoun for the subject of the gerund, it cannot refer to *Lois:*

7.69c   Lois regretted [her having seen the mess].

If Lois is the one who saw the mess, we must use the following sentence:

7.69d   Lois regretted [having seen the mess].

That is, the subject of the gerund, though understood, does not appear. Here are some more examples:

7.70a   [Your having to eat and run] worried Agnes.

   b   [Having to eat and run] worried Agnes.

7.71a   They talked about [Paul's missing classes].

   b   They talked about [missing classes].

Whenever the subject of a gerund refers to the same individual or object as a noun phrase in the main sentence, it is deleted, as the **b** versions show; it is only when it refers to someone else, as in the **a** versions, that it remains.

There are other sentences in which the subject of a gerund is deleted, namely when it refers to people or things in general, as expressed by such indefinite pronouns as *one, someone, anyone, anything,* and the like.

> **7.72a** [One's being without a car] is a nuisance.
>
> **b** [Being without a car] is a nuisance.
>
> **7.73a** The disagreeable feature is [someone's standing in the rain].
>
> **b** The disagreeable feature is [standing in the rain].

After some verbs, indefinite objects are also deleted:

> **7.74a** [One's stealing something] is dishonest.
>
> **b** [Stealing] is dishonest.

Even when a gerund phrase is reduced to a single word, as in **7.74b**, we still understand it as equivalent to a complete sentence with some of its elements deleted.

Because not all words that function as noun phrases and end in *-ing* are gerunds, let us see how we can distinguish them. First of all, gerunds are formed by adding the suffix *-ing* to verbs; therefore, such words as *spring, bring,* and *thing* are not gerunds, because *ing* is not a suffix. Similarly, certain proper nouns (*Browning, Reading*) are not gerunds. Nor are words formed by adding *-ing* to nouns: *siding, flooring, tubing, clothing.* None of these usually gives anyone trouble. But there are other words that do. *Painting* is a good example:

> **7.75a** Those *paintings* will not sell.
>
> **b** *Painting* will ruin your clothes.

Although both uses of *painting* are derived from the verb *paint* plus the suffix *-ing*, only the **b** version is a gerund. The most reliable test is to see whether it corresponds to a sentence or not. We understand **7.75b** to mean *You paint something,* but **7.75a** has no such meaning. In fact, we could substitute another noun, such as *objects,* for *paintings* in **7.75a**, but not for a gerund. Additionally, nouns may be pluralized or preceded by articles and demonstratives; gerunds may not. Here are a few additional examples, with nouns in the **a** versions and gerunds in **b:**

7.76a   Each *warning* made me more cautious.

  b   His *warning* me about the consequences made me more cautious.

7.77a   Have you read her *writings?*

  b   I regretted her *writing* that letter.

7.78a   She gave me a good *hugging*.

  b   *Hugging* strangers will get you into trouble.

Although such words as *warning, writing, hugging,* and the like may function either as gerunds or as nouns, the two uses are clearly different.

Gerunds and present participles are two other structures that look alike, and both are derived from verbs:

7.79   [Reading the gas meter] is not very exciting.

7.80   The man [reading the gas meter] is not very exciting.

These structures are derived from *one reads the gas meter* and *the man is reading the gas meter,* respectively. Whereas both appear as *reading the gas meter,* we can see that the structure in **7.79** functions as a gerund phrase; it is the subject of *is* and can be replaced with a pronoun such as *it.* In **7.80**, however, *reading the gas meter* is a participial phrase that modifies *the man.* Participial phrases can always be paraphrased with relative clauses:

7.81   The man [who is reading the gas meter] is not very exciting.

Sometimes a sentence is ambiguous, depending upon whether the *-ing* word functions as a gerund or as a participle:

7.82   [Hitting strangers] might be dangerous.

We can understand *strangers* as the object of *hitting* or as a noun modified by a participle.

INFINITIVE PHRASES

There is another structure that can function as a noun phrase: the **infinitive phrase.**

7.83a   [For Julia to become ill] would surprise everyone.

We can compare this structure with the gerund phrase:

7.83b   [Julia's becoming ill] would surprise everyone.

Like the gerund phrase, an infinitive does not contain tense. The subject is preceded by the preposition *for*, and the verb is preceded by the word *to*. Both of the above phrases are related to the following sentence:

7.83c   Julia becomes ill.

The sentence has tense, and it does not contain any of the markers of the gerund (possessive, *-ing*) or of the infinitive (*for, to*). Yet in all three we recognize *Julia* as the subject of *become* and *ill* as a predicate adjective.

An infinitive phrase can function in almost all the ways other noun phrases do:

Subject

7.84a   [For you to make a generous contribution] would please me very much.

b   It would please me very much [for you to make a generous contribution].

Direct Object

7.85   She said [for Caleb to shut his mouth].

Predicate Noun

7.86   The solution is [for you to appear bored].

As we see in **7.84b**, infinitive phrases used as subjects can be extraposed, just as noun clauses can. Also, since infinitive phrases are derived from sentences, they may contain any of the elements found in a sentence, such as subject, direct object, predicate adjective, and so on.

As is true with the gerund phrase, the subject of an infinitive phrase is deleted if it refers to the same person or object as a noun phrase in the main sentence:

7.87   It would disturb Henry [for you to pay the bill].

7.88a   *It would disturb Henry [for Henry to pay the bill].

   b   It would disturb Henry [to pay the bill].

Although the subject of *pay* is not expressed overtly in **7.88b**, it is clearly understood.

Also, indefinite subjects and objects of infinitives are often deleted:

7.89a   [For someone to read something] is [for someone to live vicariously].

   b   [To read] is [to live vicariously].

As a result of deletion, all that is left of the infinitive phrase is often just the infinitive itself. Note, however, that we understand all elements of the sentence.

After prepositions and after certain verbs, the *to* of the infinitive does not appear:

7.90   We did everything except *cry*.

7.91   He did nothing but *stand* there and look frightened.

7.92   We let Harold *do* it.

7.93   She made her mother *burn* the trash.

Otherwise these infinitives are like all others.

PHRASES, CLAUSES, AND SENTENCES

We have now seen three kinds of phrases and two types of dependent clauses that share certain features with sentences. Let us review them. First we noticed that all these structures contain the basic elements—subject, verb, complement, and optional adverbial:

7.94   The neighbors painted their house brown yesterday. (sentence containing subject–verb–direct object–objective complement–adverbial of time)

7.95   Did you know [that the neighbors painted their house brown yesterday]? (noun clause containing the same elements as the sentence)

7.96 The neighbors [who painted their house brown yesterday] aren't very friendly. (relative clause containing the same elements as the sentence, the subject represented as a relative pronoun)

7.97 I was amused by [the neighbors' painting their house brown yesterday]. (gerund phrase)

7.98 The neighbors, [painting their house brown yesterday], were unable to go to the meeting. (present participial phrase)

7.99 I didn't expect [the neighbors to paint their house brown yesterday]. (infinitive phrase)

Whatever the structure, we recognize *the neighbors* as the subject, *painted* as the verb, *their house* as the direct object, *brown* as an objective complement, and *yesterday* as an adverbial of time. In the three phrases the verb does not show tense, and it is altered according to the kind of phrase in which it occurs: with the *-ing* suffix (*painting*) in the gerund and present participial phrases and preceded by *to* (*to paint*) in the infinitive phrase. We also find variation in the subject: It is represented with a relative pronoun (*who*) in the relative clause; it is a possessive (*the neighbors'*) in the gerund phrase; and it is deleted in the present participial phrase. We nevertheless understand the same subject as we do for the sentence **7.94**.

Unlike sentences, phrases often have their subjects deleted. Participial phrases always do, and gerund and infinitive phrases do if the subject renames a noun phrase in the main clause or if it is an indefinite pronoun:

7.100a She deplored [your hitchhiking].
b She deplored [hitchhiking].

In the **a** version we see the subject *your* expressed because it does not refer to a noun phrase in the main clause and it is not an indefinite pronoun. In the **b** sentence, however, there is no subject expressed for the gerund because it is either *her or someone's*.

We can find other features of sentences within dependent clauses and phrases. A verb in any of them may be intransitive:

7.101 The tree fell to the ground.
7.102 He said [that the tree fell to the ground].

7.103   The tree [that fell to the ground] was old.

7.104   [The tree's falling to the ground] upset me.

7.105   The tree [falling to the ground] is my favorite.

7.106   He watched [the tree fall to the ground].

Or it may be transitive, taking a direct object:

7.107a   The man caught the dog.

7.108a   It amused me [that the man caught the dog].

7.109a   Did you recognize the man [who caught the dog]?

7.110a   I talked about [the man's catching the dog].

7.111a   We laughed at the man [catching the dog].

7.112a   It would be absurd [for the man to catch the dog].

Like other transitive verbs, these may become passives:

7.107b   The dog was caught by the man.

7.108b   It amused me [that the dog was caught by the man].

7.109b   Did you recognize the dog [that was caught by the man]?

7.110b   I talked about [the dog's being caught by the man].

7.111b   We laughed at the dog [caught by the man].

7.112b   It would be absurb [for the dog to be caught by the man].

Some transitive verbs take indirect objects, and others take objective complements. Still other verbs are linking, taking predicate nouns or predicate adjectives.

These five clauses and phrases differ among themselves in the ways they function. Relative clauses and participial phrases modify nouns:

7.113a   We passed by the man [who was thumbing a ride].

   b   We passed by the man [thumbing a ride].

7.114   The coat [burned in the fire] wasn't mine.

Noun clauses, gerund phrases, and infinitive phrases function as noun phrases:

7.115a   He knows *it*.

   b   He knows [that you did it].

7.116a *It* was a mistake.
   b [His leaving early] was a mistake.
7.117a I like *it*.
   b I like [to sleep late].

At first these structures may appear complicated. When we realize that they share the same features and functions as the elements of simple sentences, they become much easier to analyze.

EXERCISES

A. Enclose the noun clauses in brackets and tell how they function (subject, direct object, etc.):

1. Your silly mother thinks that this bland meal is good.
2. It is horrible that you won't help us.
3. His reason is that he can't stand you.
4. Did he tell whoever was sitting beside him the answer?
5. He will hand it to whomever he selects.
6. Did she tell you to whom she will send the letter?
7. That you are guilty is obvious.
8. He names his cars whatever he chooses.
9. Everyone is saying that you are lying.
10. It pleased us that she was so cautious.

B. Classify the italicized structures as noun clauses or relative clauses and provide evidence for your answers:

1. The belief *that John cheated* is appalling.
2. The belief *that John suggested* is appalling.
3. The suggestion *that we should wait* is agreeable.
4. We disregarded the fact *that it was raining*.
5. We disregarded the fact *that he pointed out*.

C. Fill in the blanks with *who* or *whom*, according to the rules for formal English, and tell how each pronoun functions (direct object, predicate pronoun, etc.):

1. _____ did she think it was?
2. _____ are you looking for?
3. _____ would you say stole the money?

    4. Arnold asked them _____ their sister married.

    5. Billy told them _____ had helped him.

    6. Is there any question as to _____ will succeed them?

    7. The Secretary of State is the man _____ they believe is responsible for the problem.

    8. Our helping you will depend upon _____ you pay.

    9. Your winning the election will depend upon _____ your supporters are.

    10. _____ do you think Kathy said the stranger was?

D. Enclose the gerund phrases in brackets and tell how they function:

    1. Curt's smoking his pipe in the elevator made us sick.

    2. Paul despises riding buses.

    3. Are you afraid of flying?

    4. Ellen must have given practicing Chopin her full attention.

    5. We were talking about the folly of paying one's debts.

    6. Donna's skating was amusing.

    7. She must loathe repeating her name all the time.

    8. Our favorite pastime is working crossword puzzles.

    9. Counting sheep won't make anyone fall asleep.

    10. I found cleaning ovens rather exciting work.

E. Enclose the infinitive phrases in brackets and tell how they function:

    1. Harry said for Perry to stop cheating.

    2. Their greatest ambition is to retire early.

    3. It is easy to insult them.

    4. I could do nothing except cough.

    5. To know that you are right is not enough.

    6. It is silly for you to wait any longer.

    7. He hoped to arrive early.

    8. Their plan was for Bill to wash the car.

F. Paraphrase the infinitive and gerund phrases in the last two exercises as complete sentences.

    example: Victoria wanted [to open the package herself].

                    Victoria opened the package herself.

G. Classify the italicized words as verbs, gerunds, nouns, participles, adjectives, or parts of compounds:

1. We enjoyed *running*.
2. We were *running* to the door.
3. We watched the *running* man.
4. That was a *puzzling* answer.
5. I enjoyed the *writings* that he let me read.
6. I disapproved of his *writing* the letter himself.
7. It was a *breeding* ground for mosquitoes.
8. She wore a *charming* smile.
9. He calls *writing* poetry fun.
10. He let the *sleeping* dogs lie.
11. That *infuriating* man is at the door again.
12. I gave them my *blessing*.
13. He tried to catch the *praying* mantis.
14. *Rolling* stones gather no moss.
15. *Rolling* stones is boring work.
16. I sent her a *greeting* card.
17. They were *greeting* us at the door.
18. *Greeting* people at the door is polite.
19. The man *greeting* the guests is not the host.
20. Your *greetings* do not sound sincere.

H. Classify each italicized group of words as to structure (gerund phrase, noun clause, etc.) and function (direct object, modifier, etc.):

1. We thought *that the refrigerator needed repairs*.
2. The members were talking about *inviting her to the next meeting*.
3. Did you send the people *waiting in line* enough tickets?
4. It upset me *that he laughed at my lisp*.
5. The candidate *wearing the dark coat* will probably win.
6. I believe *you are the cutest thing in town*.
7. The guest slept in the *freshly painted* bedroom.
8. *Gerald's reaching for the butter* amused everyone.
9. He did everything but *jump over the moon*.
10. Any car *that I buy* will have to be cheap.

11. *Taking cold showers* is good for the circulation.
12. It seems risky *for you to reduce so fast*.
13. I ignored the noises *they were making*.
14. The fact *that we are poor* disturbs us.
15. The fact *that upset us the most* was our poverty.
16. It is pleasant *to be praised*.
17. The people *between whom I sat* were unfriendly.
18. He enjoys *bragging about himself*.
19. We scoffed at the man *bragging about himself*.
20. Would you like *to walk barefoot over glass?*

I. Each of the following sentences is ambiguous because a word or phrase can be interpreted as being more than one structure. Explain.

1. The thought that he had proposed disturbed Emma.
2. That prim grandmother detests smoking cigars.
3. Kissing neighbors can be fun.
4. You are too big to push.

J. Write original sentences containing the following structures:

1. Noun clause introduced with *that* functioning as subject (extraposed)
2. Noun clause introduced with a WH word functioning as subject (not extraposed)
3. Noun clause introduced with *that* functioning as direct object
4. Noun clause introduced with a WH word functioning as object of a preposition
5. Gerund phrase functioning as subject
6. Gerund phrase functioning as indirect object
7. Infinitive phrase functioning as extraposed subject
8. Infinitive phrase functioning as direct object

chapter 8 ═══════════════

Movable Modifiers

In the last seven chapters we have examined two general types of syntactic relationships: subject–verb–complement structures and structures of modification. As examples of the first, we talked about the kinds of words that may function as subjects and complements, and we noticed various complements:

> **8.1** The barrel is empty. (subject–verb–predicate adjective)
>
> **8.2** They became believers. (subject–verb–predicate noun)
>
> **8.3** The doorman pushed the cart. (subject–verb–direct object)

We also looked at sentences containing indirect objects, appositives, and objective complements.

We saw further that we could embed a sentence into a noun-phrase position:

> **8.4a** Larry believes [something]. He will be elected.
>
> **b** Larry believes [that he will be elected].

8.5a We talked about [something]. You spied on Terry.

  b We talked about [your spying on Terry].

8.6a [Something] would be disastrous. Tommy tells about his plan.

  b [For Tommy to tell about his plan] would be disastrous.

  c It would be disastrous [for Tommy to tell about his plan].

In **8.4a** *something* functions as the direct object; the noun clause *that he will be elected* has the same function in **8.4b.** Both *something* and the gerund phrase *your spying on Terry* are objects of the preposition *about* in **8.5.** In **8.6** the pronoun *something* and the infinitive phrase *for Tommy to tell about his plan* function as subjects. In **8.6c** this phrase has been extraposed. Various kinds of structures may function as subjects and complements.

As for structures of modification, we saw two types. One of these is the adjectival, which can be a single word, a phrase, or a clause:

8.7 We watched the *dark* clouds. (single-word adjective)

8.8 He whistled a tune [that sounded familiar]. (relative clause)

8.9 Those people [staring at the moon] missed your stunt. (present participial phrase)

In addition, there are past participial phrases and prepositional phrases that modify nouns.

The other kind of modifier is the adverbial, either a single word or a prepositional phrase:

8.10a Henry left for school *yesterday*. (single-word adverb)

8.11a She opened the package *with great delight*. (prepositional phrase)

Some adverbial modifiers may be shifted to the beginning of the sentence:

8.10b *Yesterday* Henry left for school.

8.11b *With great delight*, she opened the package.

The positioning of such adverbial modifiers usually depends upon our concern for sentence variety and emphasis. In this chapter we shall examine a number of other modifiers that may be moved to various positions and show how this rearrangement affects the reader's ability to grasp the subject–verb–complement structure of the sentence.

ADVERB CLAUSES

In addition to single-word adverbs and prepositional phrases, there are **adverb clauses** that function as adverbials of manner, time, place, and the like. Let us start with adverbials of time:

> **8.12**   The doorbell rang *yesterday*. (single-word adverb)
>
> **8.13**   The doorbell rang *at six o'clock*. (prepositional phrase)
>
> **8.14**   The doorbell rang [while I was cutting my nails]. (adverb clause)

Like other adverbials, adverb clauses can designate time in various ways:

> **8.15**   They laughed [when they saw her expression]. (single point in time)
>
> **8.16**   He tries to trip me [whenever I pass his desk]. (habitual action)

The time of the action or state in the adverb clause may be different from that of the main clause:

> **8.17**   They had already left [before we arrived].
>
> **8.18**   They left [after we arrived].

Like single-word adverbs and prepositional phrases, adverb clauses that designate time can be replaced with *then* and questioned with *when:*

> **8.19a**   They became bored [when we showed the home movies].
>
> **b**   They became bored *then*.
>
> **c**   *When* did they become bored?

All adverbials of time—single-word adverbs, prepositional phrases, and adverb clauses—function alike. They differ only in structure.

To form an adverb clause, we add a subordinating conjunction to a sentence. Hence, we merely add a word such as *when, before, after, if,* and the like to the sentence *I fell* to produce any of the following adverb clauses: *when I fell, after I fell, before I fell, until I fell.* The list of subordinating conjunctions is longer than that of some other elements such as relative pronouns, but we can learn to recognize them easily through examples.

Just as single-word adverbs and prepositional phrases serve functions other than that of time adverbial, adverb clauses have other uses:

Place

    8.20   They are still [where I left them].

    8.21   I will sit [wherever I choose].

Manner

    8.22   He announced the guest [as we had told him to].

    8.23   Cathy smiled [as though she recognized us].

Reason

    8.24   They sold the washing machine [because they are moving].

There are also several functions of adverb clauses that have no counterparts in single-word adverbs or prepositional phrases:

Condition

    8.25   I'll scream [if you say another word].

    8.26   They won't come [unless you invite them].

Concession

    8.27   Harriet finished the race [although she had trouble].

    8.28   We will go [even if it is raining].

We could easily extend this list of types of adverb clauses, but our intention is to illustrate them for recognition purposes.

Single-word adverbs and prepositional phrases can be moved to the beginning of the sentence for variety or emphasis. Adverb clauses may also be fronted:

8.29a I will try to help [if you tell me what is wrong].

b [If you tell me what is wrong], I will try to help.

8.30a They had fled [before we could catch them].

b [Before we could catch them], they had fled.

8.31a I am moving to another room [because you are annoying me].

b [Because you are annoying me], I am moving to another room.

Unless they are very short, introductory adverb clauses are followed by commas.

ABSOLUTE PHRASES

Similar in meaning to the adverb clause is the structure known as the **absolute phrase:**

8.32a [If the weather permits], we can sleep outdoors tonight. (adverb clause)

b [The weather permitting], we can sleep outdoors tonight. (absolute phrase)

8.33a [Because her skirt was caught on a nail], she could not move. (adverb clause)

b [Her skirt caught on a nail], she could not move. (absolute phrase)

In form, an absolute phrase looks like a participial phrase that has a subject; we notice the present participle *permitting* in **8.32b,** the past participle *caught* in **8.33b.**

Absolute phrases may contain participles or any other structure that follows *be:*

8.34a [The floor being wet and slippery], we stayed outside.

b [The floor wet and slippery], we stayed outside.

8.35a [The answers being on the blackboard], we felt more confident than before.

b [The answers on the blackboard], we felt more confident than before.

Whenever a participle is not present, *being* is understood as part of the absolute phrase; we can say, therefore, that an absolute phrase consists of a subject and a participial phrase, either past or present. Like other participial phrases, this one can be active or passive, transitive or intransitive, and so on. It differs from a verb in that it does not contain tense.

Just as adverb clauses may be found at the beginning or the end of the sentence, absolute phrases may occur at either place:

8.36a [Bob having already left in the car], Carol and I walked.

b Carol and I walked, [Bob having already left in the car].

8.37a [His voice drowned out by the noise], the speaker interrupted his lecture.

b The speaker interrupted his lecture, [his voice drowned out by the noise].

8.38a [There being nothing else we could do], we laughed.

b We laughed, [there being nothing else we could do].

The choice of position depends upon emphasis and variety, not meaning.

INFINITIVE PHRASES AS ADVERBIALS

In addition to adverb clauses, absolute phrases, adverbs, and prepositional phrases, we find some infinitive phrases functioning as adverbials:

8.39a Hank came to the party [so that he could see Judy]. (adverb clause)

b Hank came to the party [to see Judy]. (infinitive phrase)

8.40a   Lorraine put on her glasses [so that she could see better]. (adverb clause)

b   Lorraine put on her glasses [to see better]. (infinitive phrase)

As with other infinitive phrases, we understand a subject that refers to the same person mentioned in the main clause; that is, we understand *Hank* as subject of *to see Judy* in **8.39b** and *Lorraine* as subject in **8.40b.**

Some infinitive phrases cannot be paraphrased with adverb clauses, as we can see in the following sentences:

8.41   Thelma looked up suddenly [to find a cat on the chair].

8.42   What can I do [to make you happy]?

8.43   He stopped smoking only [to start again].

These infinitive phrases are different from those in **8.39–8.40** in that we do not ask questions about them. For **8.39b** and **8.40b,** we have the following questions:

8.39c   Why did Hank come to the party?

8.40c   Why did Lorraine put on her glasses?

There are no questions like these for **8.41–8.43.**

Another difference between the infinitive phrases in **8.39–8.40** and those in **8.41–8.43** is that the former, but not the latter, may be fronted:

8.39d   [To see Judy], Hank came to the party.

8.40d   [To see better], Lorraine put on her glasses.

If we fronted the infinitive phrase in **8.41,** we would change the meaning:

8.44   [To find a cat on her chair], Thelma looked up suddenly.

This sentence means that Thelma's *purpose* for looking up was to find a cat on her chair, whereas **8.41** suggests that she was not deliberately looking for a cat. Her looking up merely resulted in her seeing one. Only those infinitive phrases that can be para-phrased as adverb clauses may be moved to the front of the sentence.

FRONTED NOUN MODIFIERS

Certain noun modifiers may also be moved to the beginning of the sentence when they are nonrestrictive:

Present Participial Phrase

8.45a Louis, [opening the door to the stable], let the horse out.

b [Opening the door to the stable], Louis let the horse out.

8.46a Mr. Phillips, [not knowing what else to do], sat on his hands.

b [Not knowing what else to do], Mr. Phillips sat on his hands.

Past Participial Phrase

8.47a The dentist, [caught by surprise], let the receptionist help him.

b [Caught by surprise], the dentist let the receptionist help him.

8.48a My grandmother, [attacked by a pack of angry children], screamed for help.

b [Attacked by a pack of angry children], my grandmother screamed for help.

Appositive of Two or More Words

8.49a The sea captain, [an old hand at these matters], knew instantly what was wrong with the sail.

b [An old hand at these matters], the sea captain knew instantly what was wrong with the sail.

8.50a Janice, [an especially energetic student], volunteered to give the report.

b [An especially energetic student], Janice volunteered to give the report.

Adjective with Modifiers

8.51a The baby, [sick with a cold], cried all night.

b [Sick with a cold], the baby cried all night.

8.52a Helen, [blue from the freezing wind], could say nothing.

b [Blue from the freezing wind], Helen could say nothing.

These modifiers are always followed by commas when they are placed at the beginning of the sentence.

Modifiers such as those in sentences **8.45–8.52** usually describe the subject. If they are intended to modify other words, we call them **dangling modifiers.** The **a** versions below are acceptable, but the modifiers in the **b** sentences are dangling:

8.53a Running from the burning building, Sophie carried the paralyzed child.

b *Running from the burning building, the paralyzed child was carried by Sophie.

8.54a Pleased with the paper, the teacher congratulated Mark.

b *Pleased with the paper, Mark was congratulated by the teacher.

8.55a Caught in a trap, the beaver was found by the hunter.

b *Caught in a trap, the hunter found the beaver.

Some dangling modifiers produce grotesque or confused results; others are just clumsy. Even when the meaning is clear, they are usually avoided by good writers.

EXTRAPOSED NOUN MODIFIERS

In Chapter 7 we saw that subject noun clauses are often extraposed to the end of the sentence:

8.56a [That you are so peculiar] bothers me.

b It bothers me [that you are so peculiar].

We may extrapose relative clauses in the same manner:

8.57a There was a woman [whose name was Heather] standing there.

b There was a woman standing there [whose name was Heather].

8.58a They said something [that I didn't appreciate] to him.

b They said something to him [that I didn't appreciate].

Here are examples of other noun modifiers that have been extraposed:

Appositive

8.59a The realization [that she might be the murderer] suddenly hit me.

b The realization suddenly hit me [that she might be the murderer].

8.60a I was robbed of $256, [a sum I could hardly afford to lose], by the burglar.

b I was robbed of $256 by the burglar, [a sum I could hardly afford to lose].

Present Participial Phrase

8.61a Annette, [looking for her uncle's Pontiac], watched every car that passed.

b Annette watched every car that passed, [looking for her uncle's Pontiac].

8.62a They, [not caring whom they might hurt], dropped bricks onto the sidewalk.

b They dropped bricks onto the sidewalk, [not caring whom they might hurt].

Past Participial Phrase

8.63a Carl, [stunned by the news], stood still.

b Carl stood still, [stunned by the news].

8.64a Bob, [pushed by an unknown stranger who was lurking in the shadows], fell in front of the car.

b Bob fell in front of the car, [pushed by an unknown stranger who was lurking in the shadows].

Adjective of Two or More Words

8.65a My car, [shiny after the waxing], stood in the driveway.

b My car stood in the driveway, [shiny after the waxing].

8.66a Richard, [afraid to trust anyone], kept quiet.

b Richard kept quiet, [afraid to trust anyone].

When these modifiers are long, they are usually fronted or extraposed.

THE PLACEMENT OF MODIFIERS

So far we have said little about why we move a modifier to the beginning or end of a sentence. As we look at sentences written by various authors, we can recognize a number of circumstances that may make one position preferable to another.

Good writers usually try to avoid a series of sentences that begin with the same structure unless they are being deliberately abrupt. To break up the monotony of a number of sentences beginning with subject plus verb, they look for other structures to begin some of their sentences. The following passage from "Tennessee's Partner" by Bret Harte illustrates varied sentence beginnings. During Tennessee's trial, his partner comes into the courtroom and offers the jury $1700 to let Tennessee go free. Then follows this paragraph:

> For a moment his life was in jeopardy. One or two men sprang to their feet, several hands groped for hidden weapons, and a suggestion to "throw him from the window" was only overridden by a gesture from the Judge. Tennessee laughed. And apparently oblivious of the excitement, Tennessee's Partner improved the opportunity to mop his face again with his handkerchief.

The first sentence provides a general statement about the effect of the attempted bribery. The sentences that follow describe the specific actions of various people in the room. To indicate the tension, Harte begins the sentences describing the actions with the subject in each case. By starting the first sentence with a prepositional phrase, he sets it apart and prevents the overuse of sentences with initial subjects. After the opening sentence we find the following series of events:

1. One or two men sprang to their feet.
2. Several hands groped for hidden weapons.
3. A suggestion to "throw him from the window" was only overridden by a gesture from the Judge.
4. Tennessee laughed.
5. And apparently oblivious of the excitement, Tennessee's Partner improved the opportunity to mop his face again with his handkerchief.

We might ask why Harte did not begin the last sentence with the subject because the *and* makes it look like the last item in a series:

> And Tennessee's Partner improved the opportunity to mop his face again with his handkerchief, apparently oblivious of the excitement.

Such a revision would not have been effective. The sequence of related actions actually culminates with the crisp "Tennessee laughed." The partner wipes his face, not as an act prompted by the others, but as one of apparent lack of awareness. By using different kinds of beginnings for the first and last sentences, Harte has set them off from the internal sentences. This use of sentence variety is an aid to establishing the meaning of the paragraph, not just a breaking of monotony.

A second reason for fronting an adverbial modifier is to emphasize parallel or contrasting ideas. In Steinbeck's *Of Mice and Men* we find the following:

> Crooks sat on his bunk. His shirt was out of his jeans in back. In one hand he held a bottle of liniment, and with the other he rubbed his spine.

The last sentence could as easily have been written, "He held a bottle of liniment in one hand, and he rubbed his spine with the other," but the contrast between "in one hand" and "with the other" would have been weakened. Similarly, in *The Old Man and the Sea*, Hemingway wrote the following paragraph:

> On this circle the old man could see the fish's eye and the two gray sucking fish that swam around him. Sometimes they attached themselves to him. Sometimes they darted off. Sometimes they would

swim easily in his shadow. They were each over three feet long and when they swam fast they lashed their whole bodies like eels.

The three sentences beginning with *sometimes* could have had the adverb moved to the end or between the subject and the verb, but placed at the beginning it emphasizes the parallel sentences that describe related actions.

If an adverb clause contains a pronoun or other transitional word referring to a word in a previous sentence, it is usually placed first. For example, one paragraph in Oliver Goldsmith's *The Vicar of Wakefield* ends with the landlord's departure:

At the approach of evening he took his leave; but not till he had requested permission to renew his visit, which, as he was our land-lord, we most readily agreed to.

The next paragraph then begins,

As soon as he was gone, my wife called a council on the conduct of the day.

By placing the adverb clause first, Goldsmith let the pronoun *he* come close to its antecedent. Because this clause serves as a transition between paragraphs, it is appropriately placed first. Other transitional phrases such as *in the first place* and *on the other hand* often come at the beginning of the sentence.

In other sentences we avoid ambiguity by positioning a phrase or clause in one position rather than another:

8.67a   He watched the fugitive [as he moved forward].

   b   [As he moved forward], he watched the fugitive.

In **8.67a**, the second *he* could refer to the first *he* or *the fugitive;* in the **b** version there is no confusion. Another kind of ambiguity results from adverbials that may modify an embedded sentence or the main sentence:

8.68a   Harold read the note you gave him on the bus.

Did he read the note on the bus, or did you give it to him there? That is, which of the following structures is intended?

8.68b   Harold read the note [you gave him] on the bus.

   c   Harold read the note [you gave him on the bus].

If we want to state where the reading took place, we can easily move the prepositional phrase to the beginning:

8.68d On the bus, Harold read the note you gave him.

There is no longer any ambiguity.

Another factor affecting the placement of modifiers is length. As long as subject, verb, complement, and adverbial are all short, there is no problem recognizing the structure, wherever the adverbial is placed:

8.69a Patty leaves for India *tomorrow*.

   b Patty leaves *tomorrow* for India.

   c *Tomorrow*, Patty leaves for India.

On the other hand, if any of these elements are long, their length may affect our freedom in positioning them. For example, here is how Coleridge could have written one of his sentences in *Biographia Literaria:*

> When the sonnets of Mr. Bowles, twenty in number, and just then published in a quarto pamphlet, were first made known and presented to me, by a schoolfellow who had quitted us for the university and who, during the whole time that he was in our first form (or in our school language, a Grecian) had been my patron and protector, I had just entered on my seventeenth year.

Because of the length of the adverb clause ("When . . . protector"), most readers flounder before they come to the main clause: "I had just entered on my seventeenth year." When the adverb clause comes last, the sentence is fairly easy to understand:

> I had just entered on my seventeenth year when the sonnets of Mr. Bowles, twenty in number, and just then published in a quarto pamphlet, were first made known and presented to me, by a schoolfellow who had quitted us for the university and who, during the whole time that he was in our first form (or in our school language, a Grecian) had been my patron and protector.

This, of course, is the way Coleridge wrote the sentence. After reading the short main clause, we know what the structure is and can relax while we let the adverb clause unfold. In the first version we keep asking ourselves where the introductory modifier ends.

At times it is the length of the complement rather than that of the adverbial that influences the word order, as we can see from a sentence in Charles Lamb's essay "Christ's Hospital Five and Thirty Years Ago":

> In Mr. Lamb's *Works*, published a year or two since, I find a magnificent eulogy on my old school, such as it was, or now appears to him to have been, between the years 1782 and 1789.

If the phrase "In Mr. Lamb's *Works*, published a year or two since" had been placed at the end of the sentence, the meaning would have been hazy because of the long, complex direct object.

Length can also influence the word order for noun modifiers. As long as all elements are fairly short, we have no trouble understanding the structure regardless of where certain modifiers are positioned:

8.70a   Paul, [holding his hand over his nose], ran from the room.

b   [Holding his hand over his nose], Paul ran from the room.

c   Paul ran from the room, [holding his hand over his nose].

However, when the modifier is longer, its position may affect the intelligibility of the sentence, as we can see from a passage in Hawthorne's "Young Goodman Brown." The first sentence is provided as a context.

> Young Goodman Brown came forth at sunset into the street at Salem village; but put his head back, after crossing the threshold, to exchange a parting kiss with his young wife. And Faith, as the wife was aptly named, thrust her own pretty head into the street, letting the wind play with the pink ribbons of her cap while she called to Goodman Brown.

The participial phrase "letting the wind . . . Goodman Brown" has been extraposed for a good reason, as we can see from a revision in which it follows the subject:

> And Faith, as the wife was aptly named, letting the wind play with the pink ribbons of her cap while she called to Goodman Brown, thrust her own pretty head into the street.

By the time we get to the end of the modifier, we have lost track of the structure. Good writers try to avoid arrangements of elements that make sentence structures difficult to grasp.

Finally, when a pronoun naming a specific individual has a modifier, this modifier is usually extraposed or placed at the beginning of the sentence:

> **8.71a** He, [ignoring our words of caution], went into the unlighted alley.
>
> **b** [Ignoring our words of caution], he went into the unlighted alley.
>
> **c** He went into the unlighted alley, [ignoring our words of caution].

The first version is clumsier than the other two. It should be noted that this restriction involves only pronouns referring to specific individuals. Generic pronouns—those naming people in general—have their modifiers immediately following them:

> **8.72** He [who wants to succeed] must work hard.

Otherwise, personal pronouns usually are not followed immediately by modifiers.

At times it is an author's sense of rhythm or style that dictates the placement of a movable modifier. However, the reasons given above for choosing one position over another are the ones most frequently considered.

EXERCISES

A. From the paragraph from Joseph Conrad's *The Secret Agent* given below, find an example of the following structures:

1. transitive verb	7. absolute phrase
2. intransitive verb	8. past participial phrase
3. linking verb	9. present participial phrase
4. coordinate adjectives	10. adverbial of manner
5. adjective ending in *-ed*	11. gerund phrase
6. compound noun	12. appositive

It was not a long drive. It ended by signal abruptly, nowhere in particular, between two lamp-posts before a large drapery establishment—a long range of shops already lapped up in sheets of corrugated iron for the night. Tendering a coin through the trap door, the fare slipped out and away, leaving an effect of uncanny eccentric ghostliness upon the driver's mind. But the size of the coin was satisfactory to his touch, and his education not being literary, he remained untroubled by the fear of finding it presently turned to a dead leaf in his pocket. Raised above the world of fares by the nature of his calling, he contemplated their action with a limited interest. The sharp pulling of his horse right round expressed his philosophy.

B. Some of the following sentences contain dangling modifiers. Revise them, but do nothing to the others.

1. Driving through the slush, the weather seemed worse than ever.
2. Being just a teenager, his father did not let him drink cocktails.
3. After coaxing, he decided to go.
4. The program was canceled after examining the small number of advance ticket sales.
5. To succeed on the driving test, much practice in parallel parking is essential.
6. Both the cover and the content should be considered when selecting a book as a gift.
7. Upset by the bad reviews, I vowed never to write another play.
8. Looking at the depressing list of available jobs, my decision to quit school seemed hasty.
9. By writing to the company, a person can receive a free catalogue.
10. To do this exercise, all aspects of grammar are essential.

C. Explain why the italicized modifiers were placed where they are rather than elsewhere in the sentence:

1. "*As we were thus engaged,* we saw a stag bound nimbly by, within about twenty paces of where we were sitting, and by its panting, it seemed prest by the hunters." (Oliver Goldsmith, *The Vicar of Wakefield*)
2. "*As soon as Mr. Bagshot had quitted the room,* the Count, *taking Wild by the hand,* told him he had something to communicate to him of very great importance." (Henry Fielding, *Jonathan Wild*)
3. "He went straight forward, *deviating at the church, where the crowd became thicker,* into the Rue du Faubourg

Montmartre, and so to the boulevard, which he crossed." (Arnold Bennett, *The Old Wives' Tale*)

4. "Meanwhile the men stood in calm little groups, *chatting, smoking, pretending to pay no heed to the rustling animation of the women's world.*" (D. H. Lawrence, *Women in Love*)

5. "*Before I proceed to give an account of my leaving this Kingdom*, it may be proper to inform the Reader of a private Intrigue which had been for two Months forming against me." (Jonathan Swift, *Gulliver's Travels*)

6. "*From my boyish days* I had always felt a great perplexity on one point in *Macbeth*." (Thomas De Quincey, "On the Knocking at the Gate in *Macbeth*")

7. "*On being teased by the reading and tweaked by the nurse*, the child will commonly begin to cry, which is reckoned a good sign, as showing a consciousness of guilt." (Samuel Butler, *Erewhon*)

8. "It was always a great affair, the Misses Morkan's annual dance. Everybody who knew them came to it, *members of the family, old friends of the family, the members of Julia's choir, any of Kate's pupils that were grown up enough, and even some of Mary Jane's pupils too.*" (James Joyce, "The Dead")

9. "A man's first care should be to avoid the reproaches of his own heart; his next, to escape the censures of the world. *If the last interferes with the former*, it ought to be entirely neglected." (Joseph Addison, *The Spectator*, No. 122)

10. "Tinglings of pleasure pervaded Car'line's spasmodic little frame *as she journeyed down with Ned to the place she had left two or three years before in silence and under a cloud.*" (Thomas Hardy, "The Fiddler of the Reels")

chapter 9 ═══════════

Compounding

A sentence consists of a subject and a predicate, the latter containing a verb and all required complements:

> **9.1** The manager read a letter.

The verb may be expanded with auxiliaries:

> **9.2** The manager *must have been reading* a letter.

Adverbials may be added to provide specific information about time, place, manner, and the like:

> **9.3** The manager must have been reading a letter *during his coffee break*.

And noun phrases may contain determiners, adjectives, demonstratives, and other elements in addition to the noun:

> **9.4** The *pudgy* manager must have been reading a *funny* letter during his *second* coffee break.

Even with these expansions, we still recognize the basic structure of **9.1**.

We may also combine two sentences by subordinating one to the other:

Relative Clause

9.5 We were talking to the people [who have just moved in next door].

Noun Clause

9.6 They believe [that they are being watched].

Adverb Clause

9.7 He opened the package [although his father told him not to].

Absolute Phrase

9.8 [The game being over], there was no point in our waiting longer.

Participial Phrase

9.9 [Combing the shag rug carefully], Doreen hunted for her contact lens.

Gerund Phrase

9.10 Have you considered [asking Phil for a ride]?

Infinitive Phrase

9.11 I would hate [for you to get lost].

Although both embedded and main clauses are essential to the meaning, we do not give them equal importance. In most cases the main clause expresses the principal idea, and the subordinate clause or phrase gives one that is secondary.

COMPOUND SENTENCES

Instead of making one sentence subordinate to another, we can give them equal importance. Let us start with two separate sentences that are related in meaning:

> **9.12** Ethel opened the door with her key.
> **9.13** We then slipped into the laboratory.

If we found sentence **9.13** following **9.12** in a paragraph, we would assume that the act of opening the door preceded that of slipping into the laboratory, that the door was the one to the laboratory, and that Ethel's action made it possible for us to enter. Instead of writing these as two separate sentences, we could connect them more closely by joining them into one sentence punctuated with a semicolon:

> **9.14** Ethel opened the door with her key; we then slipped into the laboratory.

However, it is only on paper that **9.14** connects the ideas more closely than the succession **9.12** and **9.13** does. We would not hear a difference if the sentence were read aloud to us. To provide closer connection, we must add a word like *and:*

> **9.15** Ethel opened the door with her key, *and* we then slipped into the laboratory.

We still have two main clauses.

It is conventional to classify sentences according to the number and kinds of clauses they contain. A sentence consisting of only one main clause is known as a **simple sentence:**

> **9.16** The attractive aborigine offered us a shrunken head.

Two or more main clauses joined together make up a **compound sentence:**

> **9.17** The attractive aborigine offered us a shrunken head, but we did not buy it.

A combination of one main clause and one or more subordinate clauses is a **complex sentence:**

> **9.18** Although the attractive aborigine offered us a shrunken head, we did not buy it.

And a combination of two or more main clauses and one or more subordinate clauses is known as a **compound-complex sentence:**

> **9.19** Although the attractive aborigine offered us a shrunken head, we did not buy it; and we were sorry later.

Most compound sentences are derived from only two main clauses, but three or more are sometimes joined together:

> **9.20** I had nothing but bad luck yesterday. My television antenna blew down, my cat got hit by a car, someone stole my tape recorder, and I forgot my wife's birthday.

The first sentence provides the context. The second is a series of four simple sentences joined into one long compound sentence. It should be noted that we did not reach a limit with four connected sentences; we could have kept adding as long as we could think of misfortunes and as long as we held the attention of our listeners.

COORDINATING CONJUNCTIONS
AND CONJUNCTIVE ADVERBS

Words such as *and, but,* and *or* are known as **coordinating conjunctions** when they join two main clauses or other structures that are alike (e.g., two prepositional phrases, two adjectives, and so on). The choice of conjunctions determines how the clauses are related in meaning.

One relationship that clauses may share is called **additive;** that is, we intend *both:*

> **9.21a** Elizabeth will invite Cathy to the party, *and* she will invite Eloise.

At times we add other words to bring out this additive notion:

> **9.21b** Elizabeth will invite Cathy to the party, *and* she will invite Eloise *also*.
>
> **c** Elizabeth will invite Cathy to the party, *and* she will invite Eloise *as well*.
>
> **d** Elizabeth will invite Cathy to the party, *and* she will invite Eloise *too*.

Or with a slight change in structure we can use *both . . . and:*

> **9.21e** Elizabeth will invite *both* Cathy and Eloise to the party.

The usual conjunction for the additive meaning is *and*.

At times *and* is used in a sense slightly different from that of the preceding sentences:

> **9.22** He hit me *and* hit me until my nose bled.
>
> **9.23** They stayed *and* stayed.
>
> **9.24** It got hotter *and* hotter that afternoon.
>
> **9.25** I tried *and* tried, but I still couldn't open the safe.

For some verbs such as *hit* this use of *and* means repetition; for others it indicates intensification.

A second relationship indicates a **choice** of one or the other:

> **9.26a** Elizabeth will invite Cathy to the party, *or* she will invite Eloise.

At times *or* follows *either* to emphasize the notion of an alternative:

> **9.26b** Elizabeth will invite *either* Cathy *or* Eloise to the party.

For negation we use *nor* or the combination *neither . . . nor:*

> **9.26c** Elizabeth will not invite Cathy to the party, *nor* will she invite Eloise.
>
> **d** Elizabeth will invite *neither* Cathy *nor* Eloise to the party.

Conjunctions that occur in pairs—*either . . . or, neither . . . nor, both . . . and,* and the like—are known as **correlatives.**

A third relationship expressed by coordinating conjunctions is **contrast:**

> **9.27** Elizabeth will invite Cathy to the party, *but* she won't invite Eloise.
>
> **9.28** I will do my best, *yet* that may not be enough.

Frequently one of the clauses is positive and the other negative, but other kinds of contrast are also possible:

> **9.29** The Pattersons are poor, but they send their daughter to an expensive private school.
>
> **9.30** He is an ichthyologist, but I enjoy talking to him.
>
> **9.31** Their daughter is over six feet tall, but she is friendly.

The contrast in **9.29** is between poverty and the ability to afford an expensive private school. That in **9.30** is less obvious, but it implies that the speaker normally does not enjoy talking to ichthyologists. Similarly, in **9.31** the speaker's opinion is that women over six feet tall are usually not friendly; this one is an exception. It should be obvious from these examples that the contrast does not have to reflect objective truth, but just the attitude of the speaker or writer.

The fourth relationship expressed by coordinating conjunctions is **reason:**

> **9.32a** We knew that it would rain, *for* we could see the clouds overhead.
>
> **9.33a** It began to rain, *so* we went inside.

These are easily paraphrased with adverb clauses with no loss in meaning:

> **9.32b** We knew that it would rain [since we could see the clouds overhead].
>
> **9.33b** [Since it began to rain], we went inside.

So is more common in conversation than in formal written English.

Closely related in meaning to certain coordinating conjunctions are the **conjunctive adverbs:**

> **9.34** We were comfortable enough in the room; *however*, we turned on the air conditioner anyway.
>
> **9.35** He couldn't hear what the speaker was saying; he, *therefore*, moved closer to the front.
>
> **9.36** I will not be finished with this novel by tomorrow; *moreover*, I probably won't be finished with it by next week.

Some other frequently used conjunctive adverbs are *consequently, nevertheless, hence, otherwise, conversely,* and *still.*

Although coordinating conjunctions and conjunctive adverbs have some similarities in meaning, they differ in where they may occur. Coordinating conjunctions always come at the beginning of the clause:

> **9.37a** He was tall, *but* he couldn't reach the ceiling.
>
> **b** *He was tall, he *but* couldn't reach the ceiling.
>
> **c** *He was tall, he couldn't reach the ceiling *but*.

This initial position also holds true for the beginning of a sentence when an idea is carried over from a preceding one:

> **9.38** *And* they never discovered the source of the odor.

Conjunctive adverbs may occur at the beginning of the sentence, but they also come in other positions as well:

> **9.39a** *Therefore*, we stopped eating in that cafeteria.
>
> **b** We, *therefore*, stopped eating in that cafeteria.
>
> **9.40a** He resigned as treasurer; *however*, he did remain a member of the club.
>
> **b** He resigned as treasurer; he did, *however*, remain a member of the club.
>
> **c** He resigned as treasurer; he did remain a member of the club, *however*.

Conjunctive adverbs function like parenthetical expressions such as *on the other hand* and *as a matter of fact.*

PUNCTUATION OF COMPOUND SENTENCES

A comma usually precedes a coordinating conjunction that joins two independent clauses:

> **9.41** He gave a long-winded account of how he was almost late getting to the theater, and then he told us that the rehearsal had been called off.
>
> **9.42** He could hear us very well, but he didn't answer.

When *and* joins two short independent clauses, the comma is frequently omitted:

> **9.43** Hal saw his mistake and he turned red.

As with introductory modifiers, there is no clear-cut line between "short" and "long" independent clauses, and practices of punctuation by educated writers vary.

When two independent clauses are not joined with a coordinating conjunction, they are punctuated as separate sentences or as one sentence with a semicolon:

> **9.44a** Snow has been on the ground for over a month, and the sun has appeared only sporadically.
>
> **b** Snow has been on the ground for over a month; the sun has appeared only sporadically.
>
> **c** Snow has been on the ground for over a month. The sun has appeared only sporadically.

The difference between using a semicolon and separating the two clauses into individual sentences depends upon how closely related the ideas are.

Like other parenthetical expressions, conjunctive adverbs are usually set off with commas:

> **9.45a** *Nevertheless*, we were eager to hear the results.
>
> **b** We were, *nevertheless*, eager to hear the results.
>
> **c** We were eager to hear the results, *nevertheless*.

Their presence at the beginning of a main clause does not affect the need for a semicolon if this clause is the second one in a sentence:

9.46a We saw that we couldn't go; we gave our tickets to Ralph and Judy.

b We saw that we couldn't go; we gave our tickets, therefore, to Ralph and Judy.

c We saw that we couldn't go; therefore, we gave our tickets to Ralph and Judy.

A safe guide for punctuation with conjunctive adverbs is to leave them out. If a semicolon is needed when they are not present, it is also needed when they are there.

When the clauses are long or if there are other marks of punctuation, semicolons may precede coordinating conjunctions:

9.47 When he learned that Daniel Calvert, his mother's brother, would be there, he still didn't agree to attend the banquet; but he sent his wife, who was a welcome guest.

OTHER COMPOUND STRUCTURES

A compound sentence may contain repeated information that is irritating to the listener or reader if it is permitted to remain:

9.48a She went to the drugstore, and she went to the library.

To remove the redundancy, we omit *she went* in the second clause:

9.48b She went to the drugstore and to the library.

The conjunction *and* now joins two prepositional phrases rather than two sentences, yet we understand **9.48b** to have the same meaning as **9.48a**. Notice that there is a comma only when *and* joins two independent clauses; there is, therefore, a comma in the **a** sentence but none in **b**.

Here are some more examples of structures other than sentences that may be compounded through the deletion of repeated material:

9.49a Harriet chuckled, and Harriet frowned.

b Harriet chuckled and frowned. (compound verb)

9.50a These coats are old, and these coats are threadbare.

   b These coats are old and threadbare. (compound adjective)

9.51a Jack went up the hill, and Jill went up the hill.

   b Jack and Jill went up the hill. (compound noun)

9.52a He wants you to stay at home, or he wants you to pay him for the ticket.

   b He wants you to stay at home or to pay him for the ticket. (compound infinitive phrase)

9.53a Sitting up straight, the child fooled his mother; and looking contrite, the child fooled his mother.

   b Sitting up straight and looking contrite, the child fooled his mother. (compound participial phrase)

9.54a They will stop working when they finish, or they will stop working when it gets dark.

   b They will stop working when they finish or when it gets dark. (compound adverb clause)

Virtually any structure may be compounded. It should again be noted that there are commas only in the **a** sentences.

We frequently find conjoined elements without a coordinating conjunction:

9.55 He resembled her other children: not overly intelligent, not very industrious.

9.56 He was consulting with his advisors, sending out requests for information, inviting experts to visit the factory.

9.57 But there were too many conflicting reports, too many figures that looked suspicious.

9.58 When the horns started blowing, when the other drivers started waving their fists, we knew that we had better get the car started.

The kind of relationship, usually additive, is not expressed overtly; the reader is expected to deduce it from the context.

When three or more items are conjoined in a series, we sometimes find *and* before each item except the first, but it usually occurs only before the last one:

9.59a The door flew open, and the telephone rang, and the dog started howling.

> **b** The door flew open, the telephone rang, and the dog
> started howling.

Some authors regularly place a comma before *and* in a series;
others omit it.

When appositives consist of a series of conjoined noun
phrases, they are usually set off with dashes or colons:

> **9.60** Everyone in the room—the Smiths, Dr. Collins, and
> the Dean—could hear what you said.
>
> **9.61** Leyden, Göttingen, and Cambridge—these are the
> universities he visited while in Europe.
>
> **9.62** She is taking the following courses: Shakespeare,
> Italian Composition, Advanced Calculus, Harmony,
> and Art Appreciation.

The colon is used only when the series ends the sentence. Also,
special punctuation is needed when the items within a series contain internal commas:

> **9.63** They rejected Paul, Rachel's nephew; my cousin;
> Robert, my cousin's friend; and several others.

The items are separated from one another with a semicolon for
clarity.

PARALLEL STRUCTURE

We may join two or more like structures, such as prepositional
phrases:

> **9.64** We looked under the rug and in the closet.

Both *under the rug* and *in the closet* function as adverbials of place.
If we try joining an adverbial of place with one of time, we produce
an unacceptable sentence:

> **9.65** *We looked under the rug and at noon.

The conjunction of two unlike structures such as an adverbial of
time and one of place is known as **faulty parallelism.**

Here are some other examples of conjoined structures that are not parallel; the **b** versions provide suggested revisions in which the same kinds of structures are joined:

9.66a   He is strong but a fool. (*But* joins an adjective and a noun phrase.)

  b   He is strong but foolish. (*But* joins two adjectives.)

9.67a   So that she could save money and to avoid eating with unpleasant people, Connie claimed that she had a previous engagement. (*And* joins an adverb clause and an infinitive phrase.)

  b   To save money and to avoid eating with unpleasant people, Connie claimed that she had a previous engagement. (*And* joins two infinitive phrases.)

The longer the structures are, the more likely we are to join two that are not parallel. In speaking, we do not always plan a sentence before we start it, but rather think of new directions as we are talking. As a result, we frequently join unlike structures. In writing, where there is opportunity for revision, we try to avoid faulty parallelism.

THE ORDER OF CONJOINED ELEMENTS

Although compound constructions are traditionally said to be of equal importance, sometimes a notion of priority is implied by the order in which they appear. Whether we address two people as *Malcolm and Norma* or as *Norma and Malcolm* may imply a degree of preference. Also, the ordering may be one of convention, such as *Mom and Dad* rather than *Dad and Mom* or *ladies and gentlemen* instead of *gentlemen and ladies*.

The ordering of some structures suggests a time sequence and a cause-and-effect relationship:

9.68   Bill saw the smoke and opened the door.

9.69   Bill opened the door and saw the smoke.

In **9.68** we assume that Bill saw the smoke before he opened the door; in **9.69** we accept the opposite sequence. We also assume that the earlier event prompted the latter.

However, when we join two structures that describe events that could not have affected each other, neither time sequence nor cause and effect is assumed:

> **9.70** Her mother was born in Canada, and her father was born in Peru.

> **9.71** Her father was born in Peru, and her mother was born in Canada.

We do not think that either birth was the cause of the other, nor do we make any assumptions about whether the father or the mother is the older. In sentences such as these, the conventional notion of equal importance for compound structures holds.

COMPOUNDING AND SUBJECT–VERB AGREEMENT

For most speakers of English, verbs agree with their subjects in a fairly consistent manner. For verbs other than *be*, the present tense has an *-s* ending for third-person singular: *he writes, she sleeps, the cactus seems*. For first and second persons there is no such ending: *I write, sleep, seem; you write, sleep, seem*. Nor is there an ending for the plural. A sample conjugation will illustrate:

I write	we write
you write	you write
he writes	they write

In the past tense there is no differentiation, regardless of person or number:

I wrote	we wrote
you wrote	you wrote
he wrote	they wrote

For the verb *be* there are additional distinctions, both for the present and past tenses:

I am	we are
you are	you are
he is	they are

I was	we were
you were	your were
he was	they were

For most people these conventions follow regularly whenever the subject is clear.

However, whenever the structure of the sentence becomes so complicated that the subject is not immediately apparent, many people hesitate over problems of subject-verb agreement; that is, for an easy sentence such as the following, only the **a** version is likely to occur:

9.72a Some snakes are in the yard.

   b *Some snakes is in the yard.

Yet when the subject is placed after the verb, as in a sentence beginning with *there*, it is no longer so obviously the subject:

9.72c There are some snakes in the yard.

This fuzziness is increased with compound noun phrases functioning as subject:

9.73a A motorcycle, a car, and a bicycle were in the garage.

   b There were a motorcycle, a car, and a bicycle in the garage.

Most people would not say,

9.74 *They was in the garage.

However, the compound noun phrase creates enough confusion over the sentence structure that a person might hesitate over whether to use *was* or *were* in **9.73**, both **a** and **b.** Once the sentence structure is clarified, the problem of the choice of verbs vanishes. Even still, compound structures with *there* are frequently seen with singular verbs in edited works:

9.75 There was no enthusiasm shown during the class and no sadness when it was over.

9.76 There is a time to make love and a time to fight.

This preference for singular subjects is no doubt a result of two factors: the length of the elements of the compound, of which the first is singular; and the use of *a, no*, or other indefinites such as *every, each*, and the like.

We normally find singular verbs with certain conjoined subjects like the following:

9.77 First her son and then her daughter was in the hospital.

9.78 Each girl and each boy was congratulated.

9.79 Every flower and every bush is to be cut down.

Also, when the conjoined noun phrases form a unit, they are treated as singular:

9.80 My friend and advisor has agreed to lend me his car.

9.81 Macaroni and cheese is not good when it is cold.

We see not only the singular verbs *has* and *is*, but also singular pronouns (*his* and *it*) referring to the combination. At times abstract nouns may be thought of as forming a unit:

9.82 Charles' love and affection for his wife was so intense that he did not suspect her of infidelity.

Some people might argue that *love* and *affection* mean the same thing; one should be omitted to avoid redundancy. Others see a shade of difference and feel that the inclusion of both words is appropriate. Although many rule books say to treat compounds such as *love and affection* as plurals, actual practice in printed works varies.

Finally, when subjects differing in number are joined by *either . . . or* or *neither . . . nor*, most rule books say that we should make the verb agree with the closer subject:

9.83 Neither her mother nor her friends were there.

9.84 Neither her friends nor her mother was there.

Many people avoid structures like this by recasting the sentence:

9.85 Her mother was not there, nor were her friends.

Similarly, when the first-person pronoun *I* is the closer subject in such a compound, the verb theoretically agrees with it:

9.86 Neither the Daltons nor I am to blame.

This can be recast as follows:

9.87 The Daltons are not to blame; neither am I.

Many people avoid structures that attract attention, even though rule books may sanction them.

EXERCISES

A. Locate the coordinating conjunctions and name the structures that they join (infinitive phrases, noun clauses, etc.):

1. Rachel did not answer any of the letters that her mother wrote her, and she even refused to read some of them.
2. She answered all the questions rapidly but accurately.
3. The old man left his children and his widow only a small portion of his estate.
4. He was embarrassed to remain in the room after confessing his misdemeanor, so he tried to slip out the door without being noticed.
5. The student whom everyone praised and who looked very promising became a recluse before she was thirty.
6. It is amusing to have everyone think you are knowledgeable but in reality not know what anyone is talking about.
7. Will you be here Monday or Wednesday?
8. Taking aspirin, resting in bed, and drinking liquids will help you get rid of your cold.
9. Your fingernails are clean, but your neck isn't.
10. Why did you watch me make that gaffe but say nothing about it?

B. Revise the following sentences to correct the faulty parallelism:

1. Martin being always in a hurry, but he never got to work on time.

2. They are people whom we not only can't stand but who insist upon having us to dinner at least once a week.

3. They vacationed in Switzerland, ate fondue, photographed Mont Blanc, the Matterhorn, the Jungfrau, went mountain climbing, skiing, skating, and hated to come home.

4. She was a good conversationalist, a fine movie critic, and served splendidly as president of the organization.

5. Ruby was quick to forget trivial insults, slow to lose her temper, and everyone respected her.

6. Thomas is not only stupid, but he is sarcastic.

7. Eunice works eight hours a day, does her own cooking, and takes care of her invalid aunt, but which does not prevent her from attending every meeting of the Serpentine Club.

8. I like to walk in the rain because of its refreshing nature and because it cools me off.

9. Although he was more intelligent than anyone else in his class, he never made fun of others for their mistakes but constantly trying to improve his own understanding of calculus.

10. He is the kind of professor always seen in hotel lobbies at conventions but who never goes to hear any papers read.

C. At times the ordering of conjoined structures can be altered without serious consequences, but at others a difference in meaning results. Comment on the ordering of the conjoined structures in the following sentences:

1. "I came; I saw; I conquered." (Caesar)

2. Would you rather go to a movie or stay home?

3. Would you like to stay home and watch television?

4. "In the spring a fuller crimson comes upon the robin's breast;
   In the spring the wanton lapwing gets himself another crest;
   In the spring a livelier iris changes on the burnished dove;
   In the spring a young man's fancy lightly turns to thoughts of love." (Tennyson)

5. "It is an ancient Mariner
   And he stoppeth one of three." (Coleridge)

6. "When shall we three meet again
   In thunder, lightning or in rain?" (Shakespeare)

7. "To Mercy, Pity, Peace, and Love,
   All pray in their distress." (Blake)

8. "I look into my glass.
   And view my wasting skin,
   And say, 'Would God it came to pass
   My heart had shrunk as thin!' " (Hardy)

9. "Stone walls do not a prison make,
   Nor iron bars a cage." (Lovelace)

10. "It was the best of times, it was the worst of times, it was
    the age of wisdom, it was the age of foolishness, it was the
    epoch of belief, it was the epoch of incredulity, it was the
    season of Light, it was the season of Darkness, it was
    the spring of hope, it was the winter of despair, we had
    everything before us, we had nothing before us, we were
    all going direct to Heaven, we were all going direct the
    other way—in short, the period was so far like the present
    period, that some of its noisiest authorities insisted on its
    being received, for good or for evil, in the superlative de-
    gree of comparison only." (Dickens)

D. Supply commas, colons, semicolons, and dashes as needed
according to the rules for standard English:

1. At the beginning he could barely stand to listen to the
   symphony but after the first movement he found it to be
   quite enjoyable.

2. His three daughters Eleanor Rosie and Penelope all answered the announcement in the newspaper.

3. Henry's older brother stood in the pouring rain a healthy
   vigorous man in his early twenties.

4. When he discovered that he had left his coat in his seat at
   the movie theater he was already halfway home.

5. Two officials namely the secretary and the treasurer have
   given their resignations to the president who reluctantly
   accepted them.

6. I have never enjoyed reading Edna Ferber's novels however I do like the movie versions of them.

7. In the middle of the street in front of our house there was
   a broken gas main so we had to leave the neighborhood
   until the gas company could repair it.

8. She wore her old yellow hat which she had been saving for such an occasion.

9. To reach my lake cottage you should go south on highway forty and exit at the intersection with Colton Avenue.

10. He sometimes reads the *Clarion* a small-town weekly newspaper that prints mostly lurid gossipy columns.

11. Her son Thomas is more trustworthy than any of her other children living at home.

12. A real daughter of her time Abigail refused to marry any man whose lips had touched liquor.

13. She had never taken a singing lesson in her life nevertheless she assaulted our nerves with her rendition of "Silent Night."

14. All I could understand were the words *apathy* and *heart* neither of which made much sense to me.

15. We were studying the play *Macbeth* Shakespeare's shortest tragedy.

16. I added the word *toothsome* which seemed to make the passage more interesting.

17. I was pleased to find the poem "To a Mouse" in the anthology even though my favorite poem "The Cotter's Saturday Night" was not included.

18. Upset by his daughter's choice of a husband Mr. Cramer was courteous and did not make a scene even though he felt like hitting the numbskull she had chosen.

19. My mother's youngest brother a conscientious scholarly gentleman advised his only son Edward to become a tramp but he decided to become a professional window washer.

20. Excited by the publicity the Helen Dawes who received all the attention didn't explain the error that had been made.

21. I feel more comfortable with the devil that I know than with the one which I haven't even met yet.

22. Your brother Frank has all the traits that I despise most pomposity aggressiveness and self-righteousness.

23. Those four cars the Chevrolet the Ford the Dodge and the Mercury will have to be moved.

24. The following students received special recognition

Louise Johnson who hadn't opened a book all semester Tony Appleton who hadn't been to more than half the class meetings and Cora Snodgrass who had cheated on every exam.

25. We could not continue to exist without the sun which is our source of light.

26. I visited my brother Martin who lives in Los Angeles but he was too busy to show me the sights.

27. The way she answered made me think of my sister Anna.

28. Those who do not work or attend class regularly will probably fail the course those who come to every class meeting however will not necessarily receive good grades.

chapter 10 ═══════════

Pronouns

Instead of referring to people or things with full noun phrases, we frequently use pronouns, especially when we do not know the identity of the people or things:

10.1 *Who* unlocked the desk?

10.2 *What* did you find in the closet?

10.3 *Someone* knocked on the door but left before I could answer it.

10.4 *Something* must be wrong.

Beyond knowing whether the noun phrases name humans or not, we have no information about them.

A second reason for using pronouns is to avoid repetition. Once we mention people, we usually do not continue referring to them with their names:

10.5a **Jim* went to the library at eight o'clock, and *Jim* stayed until closing time.

10.6a **The woman* waited in the hall, but *the woman* wouldn't give us *the woman's* name.

In each sentence we replace all but one of these noun phrases with pronouns:

> **10.5b**   *Jim* went to the library at eight o'clock, and *he* stayed until closing time.
>
> **10.6b**   *The woman* waited in the hall, but *she* wouldn't give us *her* name.

This chapter will be concerned with the uses of pronouns.

PRONOUNS AND THEIR ANTECEDENTS

In earlier chapters we saw that pronouns replace entire noun phrases, not just nouns:

> **10.7a**   *The young woman on the corner waved when we looked at the young woman on the corner.
>
> **b**   *The young woman on the corner waved when we looked at the young *her* on the corner.
>
> **c**   The young woman on the corner waved when we looked at *her*.

If we use a pronoun, it must stand for the entire noun phrase *the young woman on the corner*, not just the noun *woman*. The fact that some noun phrases consist of a single word makes it seem that pronouns at times replace just nouns rather than entire noun phrases:

> **10.8a**   *Herbert* likes *spinach*.
>
> **b**   *He* likes *it*.

However, it should be remembered that *Herbert* and *spinach* are noun phrases as well as nouns.

We speak of the noun phrase that means the same thing as a pronoun as its **antecedent**; hence, in **10.7c** we say that the antecedent of *her* is *the young woman on the corner* or just *woman*. Since the prefix *ante-* means "before," the usual place for the antecedent is before the pronoun; however, there are some exceptions, as we shall see presently.

In compound sentences pronouns never occur before their antecedents:

10.9a *He* is usually rude to uninvited guests, but *Paul* looked glad to see us last night.

b *Paul* is usually rude to uninvited guests, but *he* looked glad to see us last night.

If *he* and *Paul* are the same person, sentence **10.9a** is not possible.

When a sentence contains a dependent clause or a phrase, it is sometimes possible for the pronoun to precede its antecedent:

10.10a The speaker was ridiculing functional illiterates, even though he could barely read himself.

b *He was ridiculing functional illiterates, even though the speaker could barely read himself.

c Even though the speaker could barely read himself, he was ridiculing functional illiterates.

d Even though he could barely read himself, the speaker was ridiculing functional illiterates.

We may pronominalize the first noun phrase when it is in a dependent construction, such as **10.10d**; otherwise, as we can see from **10.10b**, the antecedent must precede the pronoun.

In gerund, infinitive, and participial phrases, we frequently find pronouns, regardless of where the phrase occurs:

10.11a Judy, trying to look *her* best for the interview, took out her gum.

b Trying to look *her* best for the interview, Judy took out her gum.

c Judy took out her gum, trying to look *her* best for the interview.

10.12a To make people like *him* better, Charles began telling jokes.

b Charles began telling jokes to make people like *him* better.

We can say that these sentences follow the same principles as those with dependent clauses, such as **10.10d,** or we can say that the real antecedent in each sentence is not *Judy* in **10.11** or *Charles* in **10.12**, but the understood subject of the participial or infinitive phrase.

When a sentence contains more than one noun, there is usually no confusion over which one is the antecedent:

10.13 Perry thanked the twins for the invitation, but *he* could not go to the party.

10.14 Randy thanked Ellen for the present, but *he* gave *her* nothing in return.

10.15 Perry thanked Randy for the invitation, but *he* could not accept *it*.

In **10.13**, *the twins* cannot be the antecedent for *he* because it is plural; *Perry, the invitation,* and *the party* are the only other noun phrases in the sentence, and *the invitation* and *the party* are nonhuman, requiring *it*. In **10.14**, as there are two human nouns that differ in sex, we know that *he* refers to *Randy, her* to *Ellen*. In **10.15**, *it* clearly refers to *the invitation*, the only nonhuman noun in the sentence. Although *he* could potentially refer to either masculine noun, the context shows that it means *Perry*, not *Randy*.

There are other sentences, however, in which confusion is possible:

10.16a Beth told Sandra that *she* would be late.

Both nouns are feminine, and the context does not rule out either one. We do not permit the repetition of the proper noun even for the purpose of clarity:

10.16b *Beth told Sandra that Beth would be late.

c *Beth told Sandra that Sandra would be late.

Some people write the antecedent in parentheses after the pronoun:

10.16d Beth told Sandra that she (Beth) would be late.

e Beth told Sandra that she (Sandra) would be late.

William Faulkner used this device at times, but for less experienced writers it is clumsy. Most people recast the sentence in a way that makes the reference clear:

10.16f Beth told Sandra, "I will be late."

g Beth told Sandra, "You will be late."

Unfortunately, there is no single solution that works for all kinds of sentences.

As we have seen in the preceding examples, pronouns agree with their antecedents in gender; that is, *she* refers to women, girls, and certain female animals. We also use *she* for a few inanimate objects such as ships, countries, and cars of which we are fond. *He* is used for men, boys, and some male animals. *It* refers to inanimate objects and to most animals. People vary in the pronouns they use for cats, dogs, horses, and cows. Some use *he* or *she* when they know the sex of the animal, especially if they call it by name, such as *Ginger* or *Ishmael*. Others use *it* for all animals. For most birds, reptiles, fish, and animals, the usual pronoun is *it*, even when we know the sex. On rare occasions we may use *it* when referring to a human, such as a baby when the speaker does not know the sex. Most mothers are not offended by "What's its name?" but they may be if they are inappropriately asked "What's her name?" or "What's his name?" Also, parents often refer to babies before birth as *it* unless they are hoping for a child of a given sex or medical tests have predicted whether it will be a girl or a boy.

When we refer to humans of either sex (e.g., *a person, anyone, a teacher*), there is no satisfactory neutral pronoun in English. For many years, *he* was considered the appropriate choice:

> **10.17a** If anyone calls while I'm out, ask *him* to call back later.

Although this practice was followed in most kinds of writing, many people did not feel comfortable with it in speech. *Him* in **10.17a** did not seem really neutral, but rather an assumption that the caller would be a male. The plural *them* was often used since it did not indicate sex:

> **10.17b** If anyone calls while I'm out, ask *them* to call back later.

English teachers gritted their teeth over this illogical use of the plural *them* to refer to one person (*anyone*). They also winced over the use of the wordy *him or her:*

> **10.17c** If anyone calls while I'm out, ask *him or her* to call back later.

Today many people accept the previously taboo structures of **10.17b** and **10.17c**. We also find others continuing to use *he* when the sex is not specified. Still others avoid the problem by recasting the sentence in the plural. Here are the possibilities:

10.18a When a person goes to the grocery store, he often finds that prices have risen.

b When a person goes to the grocery store, she often finds that prices have risen.

c When a person goes to the grocery store, they often find that prices have risen.

d When a person goes to the grocery store, he or she often finds that prices have risen.

e When a person goes to the grocery store, (s)he often finds that prices have risen.

f When people go to the grocery store, they often find that prices have risen.

g When we go to the grocery store, we often find that prices have risen.

The last two versions avoid the problems of referring to a woman as *he* (**10.18a**), sounding sexist (**10.18b**), using the plural *they* for a singular (**10.18c**), being wordy (**10.18d**), and being overly clever (**10.18e**). However, the final choice has to rest with the individual.

The acceptance of previously taboo phrases such as *he or she* provides a good example of the origin of standards. Dictionaries and other reference works base their rules on the actual usage of educated people; they do not legislate. During the period that *he or she* was gaining widespread acceptance, most rule books still recorded the older standard. Once structures such as this become accepted, reference works change their statements.

At times writers of rule books tried to formulate their rules according to what seemed logical to them rather than what educated people were using. We find, for example, the statement that if the antecedent of a pronoun is a compound joined by *or*, the pronoun agrees in gender with the closer one:

10.19 Rupert or Caroline will bring *her* book.
10.20 Caroline or Rupert will bring *his* book.

Similarly, if the members of the compound antecedent differ in number, the pronoun agrees with the closer:

10.21   The teacher or the students will give *their* view.

10.22   The students or the teacher will give *his* view.

In actual practice, few writers would use sentences such as these. Instead, they revise them:

10.23   Rupert will bring his book, or Caroline will bring hers.

10.24   Either the teacher will give his view, or the students will give theirs.

Legislative bodies may devise rules for driving cars on city streets, building houses, and smoking in public places. Most people will then follow them even if they have never done so in the past or even if the rules are illogical. Language is different in that it existed long before any rules were written down.

INTENSIVE AND REFLEXIVE PRONOUNS

English has a set of pronouns ending in -*self* that are not usually interchangeable with other pronouns:

myself	ourselves
yourself	yourselves
himself, herself, itself, oneself	themselves

Most of these are formed by adding -*self* or the plural -*selves* to the possessive: *my* + *self*, *your* + *selves*, and the like. Two are irregular. Instead of the expected *hisself* and *theirselves*, we find forms based on the objectives *him* and *them: himself, themselves*. Those speakers of English who use *hisself* and *theirselves* have regularized the forms. This is another example of standard usage being determined by the practices of educated speakers and writers, not by logic.

These pronouns are said to be **intensive** when they are used as appositives to emphasize another noun or pronoun:

10.25a   William *himself* opened the safe.

   b   William opened the safe *himself*.

10.26a   Cora *herself* will preside over the ceremony.

   b   Cora will preside over the ceremony *herself*.

Intensive pronouns agree with their antecedents; we could not use *herself, ourselves, themselves,* or any pronoun other than *himself* in **10.25.** Nor could we use any pronoun other than *herself* in **10.26.** In imperatives the intensive pronoun agrees with the understood subject *you:*

> **10.27**   Do it *yourself.*

Again, no other pronoun is possible, unless we shift to the plural *yourselves.*

Intensive pronouns may be used with nouns and pronouns that function as objects, appositives, and predicate nouns as well as subjects:

> **10.28**   We thanked the queen *herself.*
> **10.29**   We should send it to the employees *themselves.*
> **10.30**   That was the doctor *herself* speaking.
> **10.31**   Let's do it *ourselves.*

In their ability to accompany nouns in any function, intensive pronouns are like other appositives.

Pronouns ending in -*self* may also be used as **reflexives.** In this function they are usually direct or indirect objects, but they may be objects of prepositions or predicate pronouns:

> **10.32**   I kicked *myself.* (direct object)
> **10.33**   Tom and Lillie baked the pie for *themselves.* (object of a preposition)
> **10.34**   She hasn't been *herself* lately. (predicate pronoun)

Also, the antecedent of a reflexive is normally a subject, but occasionally it may serve some other function:

> **10.35**   I gave Henry the tie for *himself.*

In **10.35,** the antecedent is an indirect object.

When two noun phrases within a clause refer to the same person or thing, the second must be a reflexive unless it is a possessive:

> **10.36a** *Terry likes Terry too much.
>   **b** *Terry likes him too much.

    c   Terry likes himself too much.

    d *Himself likes Terry too much.

    10.37 Terry likes his toys too much.

Sentence **10.36a** shows that we cannot use the full noun both times, and the **b** version shows that the simple pronoun *him* is not possible if it means the same person as *Terry*. The **d** version shows that the reflexive must follow its antecedent, not precede it. Only the **c** version with the reflexive *himself* or **10.37** with the possessive *his* is possible.

These observations are also true for embedded sentences:

    10.38a I said that John cut me.

    b *I said that John cut myself.

    10.39a He said that John cut him.

    b He said that John cut himself.

Although the antecedent for *me/myself* is in the same overall sentence (**10.38**) as the pronoun, it is not in the same clause; hence, only *me* is possible. In **10.39**, if *John* and *him/himself* are the same person, only *himself* may be used. In **10.39a**, we understand *him* to mean *he* or someone else, not *John*.

When a pronoun in a gerund, infinitive, or participial phrase refers to the same person or thing as the understood subject of the phrase, the pronoun is a reflexive:

    10.40 Garland wanted [to serve *himself*].

    10.41 [To make *herself* appear taller], Sally stood on the top step.

    10.42 The woman [helping *herself* to the oranges] hasn't found the rotten ones yet.

    10.43 [Looking at *herself* in the mirror], Frances frowned.

    10.44 Their worst fault is [fooling *themselves*].

    10.45 [Belittling *ourselves*] is not something we often do.

    10.46 [Helping *oneself*] is customary in this store.

    10.47 It's no crime [to defend *yourself*].

If we did not take into account the understood subjects of these phrases, there would appear to be no system for using reflexive pronouns. In **10.41, 10.43,** and **10.45** the reflexive precedes the noun that appears to be its antecedent, yet we saw earlier that this order is normally not possible. Sentences **10.46** and **10.47** do not even have antecedents for the reflexives. Furthermore, in **10.40–10.45** what appears to be the antecedent is not in the same phrase as the pronoun. When we realize that the actual antecedents of these reflexives are the understood subjects of their phrases, everything becomes perfectly regular. Reflexives follow their antecedents, and both are in the same phrase. Even in **10.46** if we think of *helping oneself* as a reduction of *one's helping oneself*, the pronoun does have an antecedent, although understood. Similarly, in **10.47** we understand *to defend yourself* to mean *for you to defend yourself*.

These uses of reflexive pronouns have been in existence for many centuries, and virtually all speakers and writers use them in the same way, whether they are Englishmen, Scots, New Zealanders, Canadians, Bostonians, or Texans; whether they are writing a formal paper or a note on a Christmas card; whether they are arguing a case before the Supreme Court or chatting about the weather with a member of the family.

There are times, however, in which we find the reflexive *myself* where we would normally expect *I* or *me:*

10.48   "He would needs carry Will Wimble and myself with him to the county assizes." [Joseph Addison, *The Spectator*, No. 122]

10.49   The guests were received by Mrs. Martin and myself.

10.50   No one but the manager and myself knew what was going on.

These uses of *myself* without an antecedent normally occur in compounds, although they can occasionally be found by themselves in complex sentences:

10.51   Although he would have preferred to complain to someone in authority, there was no one around for him to speak to but myself.

The fact that these antecedentless reflexives occur primarily in compounds suggests that they are the result of the speaker's confusion over their function in the sentence. This assumption is strengthened when we hear people changing constructions. For example, a guide for a tour of an American city wanted the people to know that when they came out of the museum, the bus would be parked in a different place from where they left it. Either he or the driver would be available to direct them to the bus. To make sure that everyone understood, he repeated his information five or six times. He first said:

> **10.52a** When you come out of the museum, look for the driver or me.

This was changed the second time to:

> **10.52b** When you come out of the museum, look for the driver or I.

Finally, he changed to the reflexive:

> **10.52c** When you come out of the museum, look for the driver or myself.

He settled on this form for the remaining repetitions. Such antecedentless reflexives are found fairly often in informal speech, but only rarely in print other than in conversation from novels or short stories. However, the sentence from Addison (**10.48**) was included to show that this use of the reflexive is not confined to the uneducated, nor is it an innovation of the twentieth century.

PRONOUN CASE FORMS

Except for possessives, nouns in English do not change according to their use in the sentence. Whether *the electrician* is a subject, a direct object, an appositive, or a predicate noun, it appears in the same form. Most pronouns, however, have two forms other than the possessive. Sometimes these are called *nominative* and *accusative*, the terms used for two cases in such classical languages as Latin, Greek, Gothic, and Sanskrit. Because the accusative in these languages is used for only some of the functions of the English objective, we are not using this term. Instead, we shall refer to the pronoun forms as **nominative, objective,** and **possessive.** We can list them as follows:

Nominative	Objective	Possessive
I	me	my, mine
you	you	your, yours
he	him	his
she	her	her, hers
it	it	its
we	us	our, ours
they	them	their, theirs
who	whom	whose

The other pronouns in English do not change in form other than for the possessive (*anyone, anyone's*, etc.).

Except for *his, its,* and *whose,* there are two possessive forms for each pronoun. We use *my, your, her, our,* and *their* when a noun follows; we use *mine, yours, hers, ours,* and *theirs* when the noun has been deleted:

10.53a This is *my* book.

  b This is *mine*.

10.54a *Your* coat is on the floor.

  b *Yours* is on the floor.

10.55a We cleaned *her* car inside and out.

  b We cleaned *hers* inside and out.

10.56a *Their* house is older than *our* house.

  b *Theirs* is older than *ours*.

Instead of *hers, his, theirs, yours,* and *ours,* some people use the nonstandard *hern, hisn, theirn, yourn,* and *ourn,* forms patterned after *mine*. For standard written English only the forms ending in *-s* are used.

In simple sentences there is no variation among speakers in their use of nominative and objective pronouns:

10.57a *We* do not agree.

  b **Us* do not agree.

10.58a We saw *them*.

  b **We saw *they*.

10.59a   He gave *her* the money.

b   *He gave *she* the money.

10.60a   We rode with *him*.

b   *We rode with *he*.

Since *you* and *it* have the same forms for both cases, we have not illustrated them. For sentences such as **10.57–10.60**, everyone uses the nominative for subjects and the objective for the various objects for both formal and informal occasions, and regardless of the speaker's regional and social background.

When these pronouns are parts of compound noun phrases, however, not everyone uses the same forms. Let us start with the system found in most grammars as the usage of formal written English and that of most educated speakers. According to this system, compounds are treated the same as single pronouns:

Subject

10.61a   *Harold and she* will host the next meeting.

b   *She* will host the next meeting.

Direct Object

10.62a   Everyone in the office thanked *Laura and me* for our conscientious work.

b   Everyone in the office thanked *me* for our conscientious work.

Indirect Object

10.63a   You have sent *the accountant and us* the wrong forms.

b   You have sent *us* the wrong forms.

Object of a Preposition

10.64a   The project was at last completed by *the contractor and him*.

b   The project was at last completed by *him*.

When the pronoun is an appositive, it is in the same case as the noun it renames:

Appositive to a Subject

10.65   Everyone in the hall—*Terry, Claudia, and she*—could hear what you were saying.

Appositive to a Direct Object

10.66   He could see both climbers: *Allen and him*.

Appositive to an Object of a Preposition

10.67   He will mail the brochure to everyone on the list: *the thirty members, the chairman, and her*.

Appositives following *let's* or *let us* are in the objective case, agreeing with *us:*

10.68   Let's *you and me* climb this tree.

T.S. Eliot, of course, used *I* in the opening line of "The Love Song of J. Alfred Prufrock":

10.69   "Let us go, then, you and I,"

Eliot notwithstanding, these forms are the ones normally found in books, magazines, newspapers, and journals issued by reputable publishing houses. To make compounds clearer, people are often told to recast them with single pronouns, such as the **b** versions of **10.61–10.64.**

Among speakers of English there is often a great deal of nervousness over being "right." They feel comfortable with choosing pronouns for simple sentences such as **10.57–10.60;** but when they have to use sentences in which the structure is not clear, such as compounds, they are less confident. Some decide that their natural inclination is normally wrong, and they go in the opposite direction; others settle upon nominatives for all compounds as the genteel choice. Hence, we hear sentences such as these:

10.70   Between you and I, he'll never make it.

10.71   He gave it to Fred and he.

10.72   Did you see Rita and she?

Thomas Pyles in *The Origins and Development of the English Lan-*

guage cites two such examples spoken by Queen Elizabeth II and President Dwight D. Eisenhower, respectively:

> **10.73**   "It is a wonderful moment for my husband and I after nearly six months away to be met and escorted by ships of the Home Fleet."
>
> **10.74**   "I am deeply honored that so many of you should have come down to welcome Mrs. Eisenhower and I back to Washington."

Nominative forms for all compounds were at one time heard only among the semieducated. They are now found frequently in the conversation of characters in comic strips, novels, short stories, plays, and television programs. They are even heard occasionally at scholarly conventions and in English Department faculty meetings. As sentences **10.73** and **10.74** show, they may be present in the speech of British monarchs and American presidents.

Compounding is not the only process that obscures the structure of a sentence and makes the choice of pronouns confusing. Pronouns followed by appositives may be equally troublesome:

> **10.75a**   *We* committee members are overworked.
>
> **10.76a**   They gave it to *us* convicts.

In **10.75a,** *we* is the subject and *committee members* is an appositive. In **10.76a,** *us* is the object of the preposition *to*, and it takes the appositive *convicts*. The structure is clearer if the appositive is left out:

> **10.75b**   *We* are overworked.
>
> **10.76b**   They gave it to *us*.

A third cause for obscure sentence structure is the deletion of part of a clause:

> **10.77a**   We are taller than *she*.
>
> **10.78a**   Did he pay you as much as *me?*

Apparently some people tend to think of *than* and *as* as prepositions rather than subordinate conjunctions. We may expand the dependent clauses so that all understood material is included:

10.77b   We are taller than *she is*.

10.78b   Did he pay you as much as *he paid me?*

The functions of the pronouns are much clearer when understood material is provided.

Interruption of normal word order is the fourth cause for confusion over sentence structure that results in hesitation over pronoun forms. Speakers of English are so accustomed to the SVO order that they tend to equate the position before the verb with the nominative case and the position after it with the objective; in addition, they recognize the position immediately following a preposition as that of the objective. Because questions move a pronoun to the beginning of the sentence, the normal word order is disrupted unless this pronoun is the subject. Relying on the position of the pronoun in relation to the verb rather than on its function, many people use *who* in all instances, as in the **b** versions of the following sentences. The forms preferred in formal written English are given in the **a** sentences.

10.79a   Who is going with you?
   b   Who is going with you?
10.80a   Whom did they send?
   b   Who did they send?
10.81a   Whom did you leave it with?
   b   Who did you leave it with?

However, if the preposition immediately precedes the pronoun, everyone feels comfortable with *whom:*

10.81c   With whom did you leave it?

This pattern of nominative pronouns before the verb, objectives after it and after prepositions can also be seen in the **b** versions of the following sentences with relative and noun clauses:

10.82a   I gave it to the man whom you indicated.
   b   I gave it to the man who you indicated.
10.83a   Did you know whom he wanted?
   b   Did you know who he wanted?

Relative pronouns functioning as objects are often deleted in sentences such as **10.82;** there is, therefore, no problem in choosing between *who* and *whom* when there is no pronoun.

To people who are insecure about their use of pronouns, the inverted word order of questions, relative clauses, and noun clauses obscures the functions of the pronouns. Either rejecting the form that seems natural or opting for *whom* as the more elegant, they sometimes hit on the form used in standard English; at other times they overcorrect their usage, using *whom* where standard English uses *who*. The **a** versions below are the standard; the **b** sentences show the results of a consistent use of *whom:*

10.84a She is a woman whom we scarcely know.

    b She is a woman whom we scarcely know.

10.85a She is a woman who we know is punctual.

    b She is a woman whom we know is punctual.

10.86a I will ride with whom I choose.

    b I will ride with whom I choose.

10.87a They were talking about who would succeed us.

    b They were talking about whom would succeed us.

In some sentences, such as **10.84b** and **10.86b,** the selection of *whom* coincides with that of standard English; in others, such as **10.85b** and **10.87b,** *whom* reveals the speaker's confusion. For the person with only a smattering of knowledge about formal English grammar, the relative pronoun in **10.85** may seem to be the object of *know* rather than the subject of *is*. This sentence appears to be like **10.84,** in which the pronoun is, in fact, the object of *know*. Similarly, the pronoun seems to be the object of a preposition in both **10.86** and **10.87.** In the latter sentence, it is the entire noun clause that is the object of *about;* the pronoun *who* is the subject of *would succeed*. Without a clear understanding of the structure of a sentence, a person cannot select pronouns such as *who* and *whom* according to the principles of standard English.

Because of the tendency to make pronouns that are before the verb nominative and those that are after it objective, the predicate pronoun presents a special problem. Its position after the verb seems to indicate that an objective pronoun is required, yet generations of handbooks have given the nominative as the appropriate form because predicate pronouns (often called *predicate nominatives*) mean the same thing as the subject, which is nominative.

They are also nominative in the classical languages. Yet, in spite of all the hard work of English teachers trying to teach people to say, "It is I," the usual form for unselfconscious speech remains "It's me." Presumably people would use "It is I" for formal writing, but this sentence occurs almost exclusively in informal conversation. With the other pronouns some people feel more comfortable with nominatives than they do with *I*. For example, if they were identifying people in a group photograph, they might say, "This is me," but "This is he. This is she. These are they." The last sounds more normal than "These are them," but either *he* and *she* or *him* and *her* would be possible for the singulars. For one structure, the subjunctive, we normally feel comfortable with the nominative case for predicate pronouns:

    10.88   If I were he, I would consult a lawyer.

To avoid a pronoun that stands out in formal usage, either because it is too informal (*This is him*.) or because it calls attention to itself for being too precise (*This is he*.), many writers avoid predicate pronouns altogether, replacing them with nouns or rewriting the sentence:

    10.89a   It is she who should go.
       b   She is the person who should go.

The **b** version avoids the problem.

STANDARDS OF USAGE

Learning that not all speakers of English use the same pronouns is interesting, but it is not very helpful when we have to use these forms in our writing or speaking. As there are no neutral forms, we have to make a choice. We cannot write sentences like these:

    10.90   She was sitting between Gloria and $\left\{ {I \atop me} \right\}$.
    10.91   Who(m) did you think it was?

Nor can we use *between you and I* in half our sentences and *between you and me* in the other half unless we do not mind being accused of inconsistency. After learning which forms other people use, we have to decide which ones are best for us.

It would be convenient if all choices in grammar could be given the simple labels "right" and "wrong." There are, in fact, many structures for which such labels are possible:

> **10.92** Emma Bovary is not a very intelligent woman.
>
> **10.93** *A woman not intelligent very is Emma Bovary.

We can easily place an asterisk before **11.93** and say that it is not a possible English sentence. Other choices, such as when to use *who* rather than *whom*, are not so straightforward.

All of us change our manner of speaking as we move from one audience to another. At one time of day we may be in a classroom discussing Chaucer's indebtedness to Boccaccio in *The Knight's Tale*. We then go into the hall and make arrangements with a friend for a ride home. After this we stand in line at the cafeteria and talk with a stranger about the weather. When we get home, we talk with members of the family, who may range in age from two to eighty. We sometimes have to ask each person to repeat a sentence: "What's that?" "What?" "Huh?" "Pardon me?" "Would you mind repeating that?" "Sir?" We unconsciously select the appropriate term according to the other person. We cannot select one term, such as "Sir?" or "Huh?" and say that it is always the "right" way to ask for repetition.

For most situations, we have developed a high level of proficiency in selecting the proper language; in fact, we are so proficient that we can forget about our sentences and concentrate on the conversation. The ability to select the proper forms did not always come to us painlessly. As children we learned that we could refer to our mothers as "Mommie" only among members of the family, not when we were playing with other children. Sometimes we were reprimanded for being too flippant and not showing respect for our elders when we used slang or other structures, such as "Yeah" and "Nope," or the positive and negative grunts "Uh huh, unh unh." Later, when our friends asked if we were going to play baseball that afternoon, we learned that "Yes, I think I shall" was not the appropriate response. If we did not want our friends to make fun of us, we had to use one of the responses for which our elders had reprimanded us.

By the time most people are in their late teens, they are skilled in selecting the appropriate language for the kinds of conversations that are most familiar to them. No textbook or teacher can help them improve these skills. It would be unfortunate if they misunderstood the textbook statements as moral dicta to be applied inflexibly at all times. Education is misguided if it makes people ashamed of their relatives and friends or lessens their ability to communicate with them.

The real value of the grammatical rules for pronouns and other structures is in their application to those situations which are relatively new to most people: professional speaking and formal writing. If employers demand a particular standard from their employees when they work with customers, anyone who wishes to hold one of these positions has to learn to speak in the prescribed manner. For everyone the language of interviewing, selling, banking, and the like is new at first; some have more adjustments to make than others. And written English is no one's native language. People who have read widely have usually acquired considerable proficiency in the written language, but everyone who learns to write well has to spend many hours acquiring the skill. The study of grammar will not help anyone with paragraphing, developing central theses, or organizing. On the other hand, it can be indispensable in learning effective sentence structure, standard punctuation, and appropriate usage of pronouns and verbs. In many ways, acquiring the usage for formal situations is similar to learning a foreign language.

Once we recognize that there are differences in the ways people use language, how does that help us to choose between alternate forms such as *who* and *whom?* Let us look at a few examples. First, which of the following should we say?

> **10.94a** To whom did you send the chain letter?
> **b** Who did you send the chain letter to?

Since we normally want people to react to our message, not our language, we would prefer that the person addressed merely respond with the appropriate answer. If this person also reacts with "Oh, how nice! *Whom!*" or "How slovenly! Ending a sentence with a preposition!" we have created a distraction. If we are trying to develop a sense of rapport with the other person, drawing attention to our language is unlikely to serve the purpose. Sentence **10.94a** is appropriate for formal situations, **10.94b** for those that are more casual. Both are good provided they are used at the proper time.

Here is a second situation in which we have to choose between *who* and *whom:*

    10.95a   Who do you think paid for the dinner?

       b   *Whom do you think paid for the dinner?

Since sentence **10.95b** will attract attention from everyone, it should be avoided. Unlike the two versions of **10.94**, which are right for some occasions, wrong for others, **10.95b** is always wrong. It shows that the speaker is trying to use standard English but has not succeeded.

    For a third problem, let us look at a different pronoun:

    10.96a   John and I will wash the car.

       b   Me and John will wash the car.

Although sentence **10.96b** is heard more often from children than from adults, some people use it all their lives. The structure would be inappropriate for formal usage, but people should not feel guilty if they use it among friends who also use this structure.

    People who would like a simple "right" or "wrong" label for all matters of usage may feel like throwing up their hands in frustration when they are told that in a given sentence *who* is appropriate for some circumstances, *whom* for others. They may naively ask if we are not saying, "Anything goes." To the contrary, we are saying that language is more complex than they realize. In fact, we are saying that either *who* or *whom* can be wrong if used inappropriately, not that the two cases are interchangeable. In other aspects of language we recognize this kind of variability. For example, we call some people by nicknames (*Bobby*), others by full first names (*Robert*), others by titles and last names (*Mr. Anderson, Dr. Anderson*). Just as there is no single "right" form of address for all people in all circumstances, there is no single "right" use of *whom*. Human language is too complex to be described accurately with a few simple rules; people will be disappointed if they expect to find a set of rules that they can learn in thirty minutes and then apply inflexibly at all times. There are no shortcuts for the lazy.

    When we discussed variant verb forms in Chapter 3, we noted that it is only a handful of verbs that show variation among speakers of English; for the vast majority of verbs, most people use the same past-tense and past-participial forms. A similar observation is true of pronouns and other structures. After reading several pages about problem cases, a person may overestimate their importance and number. For well over ninety percent of the sentences containing pronouns, there is widespread agreement among speakers and writers.

EXERCISES

A. Explain why the italicized pronouns and nouns can or cannot refer to the same person:

1. *Larry* laughed when *he* heard the announcement.
2. Because *she* was in such a rush, *Lottie* forgot her car keys.
3. *She* kicked the man who ridiculed *Dollie*.
4. Anyone who wants *them* may have *these cookies*.
5. *They* are especially courteous to anyone who leaves *those waiters* a big tip.

B. Replace the italicized noun phrases with pronouns that are appropriate for formal written English. If a sentence sounds artificial, revise it to avoid the problem.

1. In this world a person must do everything *a person* can to fight intolerance.
2. We invited everyone at the office to our Christmas party, and we hope *everyone at the office* can come.
3. Jeannie or I will let you see *Jeannie's* or my answers.
4. A member of the faculty wives' club announced that *a member of the faculty wives' club* would make the speech. [NB: The member who made the announcement is the one who will make the speech.]
5. Neither of the men will promise *neither of the men's* support.

C. In each of the following sentences, the italicized pronouns and nouns are supposed to refer to the same person. Explain what is wrong with the sentences marked with an asterisk; do not just correct them. Also explain why the choices of pronouns in the other sentences are correct.

1. *Nicole* is in love with *herself*.
2. **Those boys* invited *himself* to the party.
3. **Themselves* outsmarted *those men*.
4. *I saw* no one in the mirror except *myself*.
5. **I* detested the girl sitting behind *myself*.
6. *Charles* was told to protect *himself*.
7. Finding *herself* without any money didn't worry *Janice*.
8. **Ann told *Frank* that it would be disastrous to marry *himself*.

9. *Paul* was believed to have cheated *him*.

10. *Congratulating *yourself* will make people despise *yourself*.

D. Locate the reflexive pronouns in the following passage from James Boswell's *Life of Samuel Johnson* and explain how they follow the rules for reflexives given in this chapter:

> When we entered Mr. Dilly's drawing room, he [i.e., Johnson] found himself in the midst of a company he did not know. I kept myself snug and silent, watching how he would conduct himself. I observed him whispering to Mr. Dilly, "Who is that gentleman, Sir?"—"Mr. Arthur Lee."—JOHNSON, "Too, too, too" (under his breath), which was one of his habitual mutterings. . . . "And who is the gentleman in lace?"—"Mr. Wilkes, Sir." This information confounded him still more; he had some difficulty to restrain himself, and taking up a book, sat down upon a window seat and read, or at least kept his eye upon it intently for some time, till he composed himself.

E. Select pronouns that are appropriate for formal written English:

1. The stage manager and (she/her/herself) should have arranged those details.
2. Will they send it to you or (I/me)?
3. They opened the exhibit especially for (we/us) tennis players.
4. No one worked harder than (they/them/themselves).
5. The announcement pleased no one more than (he/him/himself).
6. Did they give you and (she/her) anything to eat?
7. He never had a kind word for my brother or (I/me/myself).
8. Was she the actress (who/whom) you read about?
9. Polly is the contestant (who/whom) everyone thinks will be chosen.
10. Who does he think wrote the note, Jenkins or (I/me/myself)?
11. The artist thanked Gerald and (he/him) for being so patient.
12. Would you apologize if you were (she/her)?
13. Can you sing as well as (he/him)?
14. The audience and (we/us) card players were all asked to leave immediately.

15. He shouted at (we/us) swimmers.
16. Everyone who tries to be nice to her—even her uncle and (I/me/myself)—is treated rudely.
17. Just between you and (I/me/myself), her poetry is miserable.
18. I have bought a box lunch for Cal and (I/me/myself).
19. She was sitting behind the losers, (he/him) and (I/me/myself).
20. (Who/whom) did you say they think should be fired?

F. Write *Acceptable* before those sentences that are appropriate for formal written English. Explain which changes are needed to make the others acceptable for this level of usage.

1. Noboby but him is interested in who is to be assigned the chairmanship.
2. The river had already overflown before we thought about who might still be in the house.
3. Do every one of you have a ride for tonight?
4. The new mayor is one of the most corrupt politicians that have ever been elected in this city.
5. He is the one whom everyone believed would finish last.
6. Every one of the women had requested some special pencils for their own use.
7. She wanted to have some free time so that she could lay in the sun for a few hours.
8. We have heard that neither the teachers nor the Dean is in favor of the new salary scale.
9. They tried to make it appear that we children were responsible for the confusion.
10. How could a simple boy like him refuse?
11. They could have beat the other team if they had been rested.
12. Which one of us did you want to see, Richard or me?
13. The English Building as well as all other buildings on that side of the campus was to be torn down.
14. Are you saying that she can type as fast as Lonnie or me?
15. The completion of the invitations and program guides have been more time consuming than anyone had realized.

16. She said that the ship sunk before everyone was rescued.
17. Has she showed you the new Administration Building?
18. Did you know that there is a man in a heavy overcoat and a woman in shorts waiting outside?
19. There, looking frightened, were the old woman and her six children.
20. Everyone in the class sat there looking as though they had never heard of Ruskin.

G. Assume that the following sentences are intended for conversation among professional people who speak standard English and also want to be cordial. Classify each sentence as appropriate, nonstandard, or pretentious.

1. He said that the house was for the use of Jack and I.
2. Anyone who agrees to work overtime should have their salary frozen.
3. I'm next on the list, aren't I?
4. I don't know about what you are talking.
5. The result of the investigations were that Compton was proved innocent.
6. He asked why I done it, but I didn't answer.
7. I, too. [Response to "I'm going to each lunch in the cafeteria downstairs."]
8. The policeman told Harold and me to go home.
9. Whomever you nominate will be elected.
10. Who do you think I should send it to?

chapter 11 ═══════════════

Sentence Structure and Complexity

In the last three chapters we noticed that some sentences are more difficult to understand than others. In Chapter 8, we said that a sentence may be clearer if a modifier is placed in one position rather than in another. Then in Chapters 9 and 10 we saw that compounding can obscure the structure so that people write phrases and clauses that are not parallel or hesitate over which pronoun to use. It seems appropriate, then, that this final chapter should review the ways in which sentence structure can increase or reduce complexity.

There are features other than sentence structure that make some sentences more difficult to understand than others, but they lie outside the scope of this book. For example, two accounts of the weather would differ considerably if one were written by a meteorologist and the other by a nonspecialist. Both might describe conditions during the same days, but the content and vocabulary would not be the same.

Also, some literary passages are harder for certain readers than for others. Shakespeare's sonnets, for example, are not especially difficult for the person accustomed to reading poetry; but to the student whose past exposure to poetry has been limited to works on the level of Joyce Kilmer's "Trees," those same sonnets may seem like something written in a foreign language. Many scholars have noticed that they had to learn to read certain writers almost the way they would another language: Henry James, William Faulkner, Gerard Manley Hopkins, William Butler Yeats, to name just a few. Yet those people who have spent many hours reading these writers and learned to appreciate them find them much less formidable because of the skills they have developed. They are like athletes who can do thirty push-ups without beginning to breathe heavily, whereas people in poor physical condition might find anything over five impossible.

As we speak of certain sentences being more complex than others, we do not mean that the good reader necessarily has trouble understanding them. The following sentences, for example, are presented in an order of increasing complexity:

11.1 "Tom touched his father on the shoulder." [John Steinbeck, *The Grapes of Wrath*]

11.2 "The town itself is dreary; not much is there except the cotton mill, the two-room houses where the workers live, and a few peach trees, a church with two colored windows, and a miserable main street only a hundred yards long." [Carson McCullers, *The Ballad of the Sad Cafe*]

11.3 "The fixer hurriedly travels on the train to Minsk and after months of desperate searching meets the old man, the moon on his rabbinic hat, coming home one evening from the synagogue." [Bernard Malamud, *The Fixer*]

11.4 "It was the summer after that first Christmas that Henry brought him home, the summer following the two days of that June vacation which he spent at Sutpen's Hundred before he rode on to the river to take the steamboat home, that summer after my aunt left and papa had to go away on business and I was sent out to Ellen (possibly my father chose Ellen as a refuge for me because at that time Thomas Sutpen was also absent) to stay so that she could take care of me, who had been born too late, born into some curious disjoint of my father's life and left on his (now twice) widowed hands, I competent enough to reach a kitchen shelf, count

spoons and hem a sheet and measure milk into a
churn yet good for nothing else, yet still too valuable to be left alone." [William Faulkner, *Absalom,
Absalom!*]

Although the easiest sentence in this group is the shortest and the
hardest is the longest, length alone is not the cause of the difficulty.
To the person who has learned to read Faulkner, all four passages
are comprehensible, and even the last requires no great strain. The
differences among them are similar to those of the athletes who do
five, ten, fifteen, or thirty push-ups. Although they can do any of
these numbers, it still takes more effort to do thirty than it does to
do five.

DISRUPTION OF THE SVO ORDER

The easiest sentences are those that are in the normal SVO order
and that have no embedded or compound structures. There are
several common processes that rearrange order, as the following
sentences illustrate:

11.5   There were some ants in the breadbox.

11.6   Never have I heard anything so silly.

11.7   Whom did you tell?

Provided that the sentences are short, alterations of the SVO order
such as these increase the complexity of the sentences only
slightly; however, the fact that some people have trouble deciding
whether to use a singular or plural verb in sentence **11.5** and *who*
or *whom* in **11.7** shows that they are more difficult than the simple
declaratives with SVO order.

Rearrangements of word order for poetry also make sentences
less straightforward. For example, the opening line of Robert
Frost's "Stopping by Woods on a Snowy Evening" has an inversion:

11.8a   "Whose woods these are I think I know."

The normal order would have been:

11.8b   I think I know whose woods these are.

The line as Frost wrote it is obviously better poetry than the revision, but it is also less simple and may give trouble to the student who does not read well.

Let us compare a few lines from two poems to see how they differ in word order. Keats's sonnet "On First Looking into Chapman's Homer" begins like this:

> Much have I traveled in the realms of gold,
> And many goodly states and kingdoms seen;
> Round many western islands have I been
> Which bards in fealty to Apollo hold.

Since the poem describes an emotional response, it is rich in poetic diction and imagery. However, it is not just the choice of words and the allusions that set the tone; the word order is different from that found in prose. If we were asked to paraphrase the first four lines, keeping the same diction and imagery, we could write something like this:

> I have traveled much in the realms of gold,
> And seen many goodly states and kingdoms;
> I have been round many western islands
> Which bards hold in fealty to Apollo.

The lines no longer rhyme, and the meter has been changed for the worse; the content and imagery remain the same. What we have done is to revise the word order to that of Modern English prose so that a person who has not understood the lines will find them easier. In the first line we moved the adverb *much* after the verb *traveled* and positioned the subject before the verb, producing the following order:

Subject–Verb–Adverb of Frequency–Adverb of Place

In the second we placed the verb *seen* before its object. We made similar adjustments in the last two lines.

By contrast, Robert Frost's poem "The Death of the Hired Man" seems more commonplace:

> Mary sat musing on the lamp-flame at the table
> Waiting for Warren. When she heard his step,
> She ran on tip-toe down the darkened passage

To meet him in the doorway with the news
And put him on his guard. 'Silas is back.'

We notice an absence of poetic diction and mythological allusions, as is appropriate for lines describing simple physical actions. If we were asked to paraphrase these lines the way we did those by Keats, we would probably not be able to write anything simpler. The normal word order for Modern English prose is already present. This is one of the reasons that this poem by Frost seems easier than the sonnet by Keats.

EMBEDDED SENTENCES

Another source of sentence complexity is the presence of embedded sentences. Like the athletes who do a few push-ups, we hardly notice certain kinds of embedding:

>   **11.9**   When Roger took off his coat, we could see that he had been sweating.

Other kinds make sentences difficult to understand, and at times even incomprehensible. For example, we can start with a simple sentence like this:

>   **11.10**   The doctor frowned.

To explain which doctor we mean, we can introduce a relative clause based on the sentence *The patient hit the doctor:*

>   **11.11a**   The doctor that the patient hit frowned.
>   **b**   The doctor the patient hit frowned.

The sentence is slightly easier with the relative pronoun included, as in **11.11a**, but both versions **a** and **b** are more difficult than **c:**

>   **11.11c**   The doctor who was hit by the patient frowned.

Sentence **11.11b** is hard to understand but not impossible. If we add a relative clause to tell which patient did the hitting, based on *The nurse poked the patient*, the result is beyond the comprehension of most people:

11.12a The doctor the patient the nurse poked hit frowned.

If we revise the sentence to break up the series of three nouns followed by three verbs, the sentence is understandable:

11.12b The doctor who was hit by the patient that was poked by the nurse frowned.

  c The doctor frowned who was hit by the patient that the nurse poked.

It is not just embedding by itself that makes a sentence complicated; it is the kind of embedding.

Sentence **11.12c** illustrates a device that we often use to make sentences easier: extraposition. It would seem that this device would have the opposite effect because it moves some element, often the subject, out of its normal SVO position. However, for very long structures extraposition helps us to understand the sentence, as in the following example:

11.13a "That when the Erewhonians profess themselves to be quite certain about any matter, and avow it as a base on which they are to build a system of practice, they seldom quite believe in it is a distinguishing peculiarity of the Erewhonians."

In this arrangement with the long subject noun clause in initial position, everyone finds the sentence virtually impossible. If we extrapose the subject noun clause, as Samuel Butler did in *Erewhon*, the sentence becomes clear:

11.13b "It is a distinguishing peculiarity of the Erewhonians that when they profess themselves to be quite certain about any matter, and avow it as a base on which they are to build a system of practice, they seldom quite believe in it."

We also changed the instance of *the Erewhonians* to *they* in keeping with the rules for pronominalization, but this has nothing to do with sentence complexity. By extraposing the subject, we marked out the structure, using the filler *it*. After indicating the structure, we then gave the long subject.

INTERRUPTIONS

Another means of changing the expected SVO order is to insert adverbials or parenthetical phrases within the sentence. For short sentences such interruptions are barely noticeable:

11.14a *Next fall*, Albert will open a restaurant.
   b Albert will open a restaurant *next fall*.
   c Albert, *next fall*, will open a restaurant.

Even for short sentences adverbials that interrupt, as in the **c** version, make the sentences less natural than others such as **a** and **b.**

When the sentences are longer, such interruptions tend to make them more difficult. The following passage is from "The Tree of Knowledge" by Henry James, a writer who was fond of such interrupting devices:

> It was one of the secret opinions, such as we all have, of Peter Brench that his main success in life would have consisted in his never having committed himself about the work, as it was called, of his friend Morgan Mallow. This was a subject on which it was, to the best of his belief, impossible with veracity to quote him, and it was nowhere on record that he had, in the connexion, on any occasion and in any embarrassment, either lied or spoken the truth.

Such as we all have comes between the noun *opinions* and its modifying prepositional phrase *of Peter Brench*. A similar clause, *as it was called*, separates *the work* from *of his friend Morgan Mallow*. Later, *to the best of his belief* separates the verb *was* from the predicate adjective *impossible*. And the long phrase *in the connexion, on any occasion and in any embarrassment* comes between the auxiliary *had* and its verb. The passage is less straightforward than it would have been if the order of the basic sentence elements had been left intact. We also notice the adverbial phrase *with veracity* preceding the infinitive *to quote*, rather than coming in the more basic order *to quote him with veracity*. James's positioning of adverbials and parenthetical phrases is one of the features that produce the effect readers describe as "complex" and "convoluted." To the person reading James for the first time, the word order may seem eccentric. After several readings of a short story such as "The Tree of Knowledge," however, the same reader usually comes to realize that although James's reasons for placing each phrase where he did are not always obvious, the story would suffer if they were changed.

Let us take another sentence from the same short story to see exactly what James did with it. We start with a simple sentence:

> **11.15a**   Mrs. Mallow broke the news to their friend one day.

We next add an adverb clause to specify the day more exactly:

> **11.15b**   Mrs. Mallow broke the news to their friend one day *when the boy was turning twenty*.

Now let us add a relative clause to modify *their friend:*

> **11.15c**   Mrs. Mallow broke the news to their friend, *who shared their problems and pains*, one day when the boy was turning twenty.

The sentence is more complicated now, but we can still understand it with no difficulty. Let us next give the degree to which he shared the problems and pains: *to the last delicate morsel.*

> **11.15d**   Mrs. Mallow broke the news to their friend, who shared their problems and pains *to the last delicate morsel*, one day when the boy was turning twenty.

With the long modifier for *friend*, the adverbial of time does not seem quite right at the end. We could move it to the beginning of the sentence:

> **11.15e**   *One day when the boy was turning twenty*, Mrs. Mallow broke the news to their friend, who shared their problems and pains to the last delicate morsel.

However, this would not be in accordance with James's style. Instead, let us place this adverbial modifier between the subject and verb:

> **11.15f**   Mrs. Mallow, *one day when the boy was turning twenty*, broke the news to their friend, who shared their problems and pains to the last delicate morsel.

And let us move *to the last delicate morsel* between the verb *shared* and its object:

> **11.15g**   Mrs. Mallow, one day when the boy was turning twenty, broke the news to their friend, who shared, *to the last delicate morsel*, their problems and pains.

With the last two rearrangements (**11.15f** and **11.15g**), we have made the sentence more complicated than the **e** version, yet **g** sounds more like James than **e** does.

But we are not through. Let us explain what the news is: *that it seemed as if nothing would really do but that he should embrace the career*. Instead of *the news*, let us use this noun clause:

> **11.15h**   Mrs. Mallow, one day when the boy was turning twenty, broke *that it seemed as if nothing would really do but that he should embrace the career* to their friend, who shared, to the last delicate morsel, their problems and pains.

Although James is often difficult, he is not unreadable. Let us, then, extrapose the object noun clause and fill its position with the expletive *it:*

> **11.15i**   "Mrs. Mallow, one day when the boy was turning twenty, broke it to their friend, who shared, to the last delicate morsel, their problems and pains, that it seemed as if nothing would really do but that he should embrace the career."

We now have James's sentence.

HEMINGWAY AND CONRAD

If we examine a passage by Hemingway and another by Conrad, we notice that Hemingway's style seems easier than Conrad's. First, Hemingway:

> He felt of his knee. The pants were torn and the skin was barked. His hands were scraped and there were sand and cinders driven up under his nails. He went over to the edge of the track down the little slope to the water and washed his hands. He washed them carefully

in the cold water, getting the dirt out from the nails. He squatted down and bathed his knee.

Then Conrad:

> It must be explained here that my cabin had the form of the capital letter L the door being within the angle and opening into the short part of the letter. A couch was to the left, the bed-place to the right; my writing-desk and the chronometers' table faced the door. But any one opening it, unless he stooped right inside, had no view of what I call the long (or vertical) part of the letter. It contained some lockers surmounted by a bookcase; and a few clothes, a thick jacket or two, caps, oilskin coat, and such like, hung on hooks. There was at the bottom of that part a door opening into my bath-room, which could be entered also directly from the saloon. But that way was never used.

The first difference that we notice is the length of the sentences. There are six sentences in each passage, but whereas the first contains only 71 words, the second has 131—almost twice as many. We find a similar ratio if we compare the average number of words in the sentences of the two passages:

Hemingway Sentence	Words	Conrad Sentence	Words
1	5	1	31
2	9	2	20
3	15	3	25
4	20	4	26
5	15	5	23
6	7	6	6
Total	71	Total	131

The average number of words per sentence in the Hemingway passage is twelve, that in the Conrad twenty-two, again a ratio of almost 2:1. However, Hemingway does have some longer sentences, the fourth coming almost to Conrad's average; and Conrad's last sentence is shorter than most of those in the Hemingway passage. Yet even Hemingway's longer sentences seem much simpler than those by Conrad.

If we turn from length to the kinds of structures found in the sentences by the two writers, we see a major difference. Let us compare the embedded phrases and clauses:

Hemingway Sentence	Embedding
1	0
2	0
3	Past participial phrase
4	0
5	Present participial phrase
6	0

There are only two participial phrases in the Hemingway passage, no other phrases or clauses. In the Conrad passage we find more:

Conrad Sentence	Embedding
1	Noun clause, Absolute phrase (compound)
2	Absolute phrase
3	Present participial phrase, Adverb clause, Noun clause
4	Past participial phrase, Past participial phrase
5	Present participial phrase, Relative clause
6	0

Only the last sentence has no embedded structures; there are ten in the other five. In the Conrad passage most sentences have at least two embedded clauses or phrases, and in the fifth sentence the relative clause is embedded within the present participial phrase. In addition to the number of embedded structures, there is a rich variety. Whereas Conrad achieved his sentence length through embedding, Hemingway got his mainly through compounding (sentences two and three) or joining prepositional phrases (sentence four). It is the kinds of structures used by the authors that make their styles seem easy or complex, not the length of the sentences alone.

If we are talking about directions on a medicine bottle or similar uses of language, simpler sentences are preferable to the more complex, as long as both convey the same information. For other purposes, however, the simple style may not always be the better. If most people tried to write in Hemingway's style, the result would sound choppy and childish. No one is interested in reading an account of modern problems in politics, the arts, or education if it sounds as though a child wrote it. Style can detract from the content to the point that people do not weigh the ideas.

Hemingway was extremely successful in adapting his style to his content in a way that does not sound childish. If the content of a novel by Faulkner, James, or Conrad were attempted in a style such as Hemingway's, it is doubtful that anyone would care to read it. There are a great many intangible features that determine which style is best, not ease or complexity alone.

EXERCISES

A. Sentences **11.1–11.4** are listed in an order of increasing complexity. Explain what makes each one harder than the one before.

B. In this chapter we compared a passage from Hemingway with one from Conrad and explained why the latter seems more complex than the former. Make a similar comparison between the Conrad passage and the one from James quoted earlier in this chapter.

C. Read each of the following passages and classify it as easy, moderately difficult, or difficult. Then comment on the sentence structure to justify your classification.

   1. Tom Willard went briskly along the hallway and down a flight of stairs to the office. The woman in the darkness could hear him laughing and talking with a guest who was striving to wear away a dull evening by dozing in a chair by the office door. She returned to the door of her son's room. The weakness had passed from her body as by a miracle and she stepped boldly along. A thousand ideas raced through her head. When she heard the scraping of a chair and the sound of a pen scratching upon paper, she again turned and went back along the hallways to her own room. [Sherwood Anderson, *Winesburg, Ohio*]

   2. As, in gaining his place, some little perseverance, not to say persistence, of a mildly inoffensive sort, had been unavoidable, it was not with the best relish that the crowd regarded his apparent intrusion; and upon a more attentive survey, perceiving no badge of authority about him, but rather something quite the contrary—he being of an aspect so singularly innocent; an aspect, too, which they took to be somehow inappropriate to the time and

place, and inclining to the notion that his writing was of much the same sort: in short, taking him for some strange kind of simpleton, harmless enough, would he keep to himself, but not wholly unobnoxious as an intruder—they made no scruple to jostle him aside. [Herman Melville, *The Confidence Man*]

3. And the aged lord, without a word, shambled silently away, his old velvet shoes flapping and off at his heels, coughing as he went. As for Wang Lung, left alone with this woman, he did not know what to say or do. He was stupefied with the silence everywhere. He glanced into the next court and still there was no other person, and about the court he saw heaps of refuse and filth and scattered straw and branches of bamboo trees and dried pine needles and the dead stalks of flowers, as though not for a long time had anyone taken a broom to sweep it. [Pearl S. Buck, *The Good Earth*]

4. By ten-forty-five it was all over. The town was occupied, the defenders defeated, and the war finished. The invader had prepared for this campaign as carefully as he had for larger ones. On this Sunday morning the postman and the policeman had gone fishing in the boat of Mr. Corell, the popular storekeeper. He had lent them his trim sailboat for the day. The postman and the policeman were several miles at sea when they saw the small, dark transport, loaded with soldiers, go quietly past them. As officials of the town, this was definitely their business, and these two put about, but of course the battalion was in possession by the time they could make port. The policeman and the postman could not even get into their own offices in the Town Hall, and when they insisted on their rights they were taken prisoners of war and locked up in the town jail. [John Steinbeck, *The Moon Is Down*]

5. The affair being brought to this head, Mr. George, after a little consideration, proposed to go in first to his comrade (as he called him), taking Miss Flite with him. Mr. Bucket agreeing, they went away to the further end of the gallery, leaving us sitting and standing by a table covered with guns. Mr. Bucket took this opportunity of entering into a little light conversation, asking me if I were afraid of fire-arms, as most young ladies were; asking Richard if he

were a good shot; asking Phil Squod which he considered the best of those rifles and what it might be worth first-hand, telling him in return that it was a pity he ever gave way to his temper, for he was naturally so amiable that he might have been a young woman, and making himself generally agreeable. [Charles Dickens, *Bleak House*]

Appendix:
Parts of Speech

As a person who speaks, reads, and writes English, you already know a great deal about grammar. For example, you are able to say that certain substitutions are possible but others are not. Try replacing *car* in the following sentence with each of the words in the groups below:

My *car* is outside.

A	B	C
ball	leg	quickly
grandmother	happiness	of
chair	courage	and
guest	anger	could

The words under *A* easily replace *car*. You may have to pause for those under *B*, but with a little imagination you can think of contexts in which they fit; the problem is their meaning, not the kind of words they are. The words under *C*, however, are the wrong kind to replace *car*. You would be able to make these judgments even if you had never heard the words *noun, verb, adjective, preposition,* or *conjunction*. But if you know the meanings of these grammatical terms and are able to classify words into the categories they name, you can make a precise statement about why the words in groups *A* and *B* are possible replacements for *car*: They are nouns. Similarly, those under *C* are unsatisfactory replacements because they are not nouns. To illustrate the value of these terms and the concepts they name, try explaining why *quickly* or *of* cannot replace *car* without using words such as *noun, adverb,* or *preposition*. Also, avoid using the definitions for these words.

People who study language use the word *grammar* in various ways. The first is the knowledge we have that permits us to construct and understand sentences; it also allows us to make judgments about sentences, such as you did when you said that *could* is not a possible substitution for *car*. This grammar is called **internalized grammar.** It is this grammar that makes the study of English sentences easier for you than such totally new subjects as calculus or economics. The second kind of grammar is the one you find in books. It classifies words as to parts of speech, defines functions such as objects and subjective complements, and shows how words are grouped into phrases and clauses. When we need to distinguish it from other grammars, we call it **formal grammar.** Finally, there is a third kind of grammar: the one that evaluates words and structures as standard or nonstandard English. This kind of grammar is more commonly referred to as **usage.** It is the second type, formal grammar, that you are studying in this book, but you are using your internalized grammar to make learning easier and to evaluate the statements that are made. You then use formal grammar to help make decisions about usage and punctuation.

One of the most fundamental classifications in grammar is that of words into the eight parts of speech: **noun, pronoun, verb, adjective, adverb, preposition, conjunction, interjection.** When you determined which words could replace *car* in *My car is outside*, you were using this information. A classification of this type has existed in the grammars of various languages since the time of the ancient Greeks, although not all grammarians have made the same divisions. When we say that this classification is fundamental, we mean that it is the basis on which we classify clauses and phrases as well as words. We also rely upon parts of speech when we discuss the ways words function in sentences and when we decide whether to use one word or another in a given sentence, such as "You played *good*" or "You played *well*."

It would be natural to assume that good definitions exist for ideas that have been in existence for over two thousand years. Unfortunately, this is not the case. Some of the conventional definitions for parts of speech are too vague to be of much use, and others overlap with each other. During the last fifty years, there have been a number of attempts to redefine, regroup, and even rename the parts of speech. Although none of the attempts have succeeded in providing a system that holds up under continued use, they have given us much insight into the ways words are grouped. In the discussion that follows, we will use the traditional eight parts of speech: noun, pronoun, verb, adjective, adverb, preposition, conjunction, and interjection. We will state the usual definitions but supplement them with other devices that have been suggested by linguists of this century. Finally, we will look at examples and decide how we classify a given word as a noun, adjective, verb, and so on.

NOUNS

A **noun** is the name of a person, place, thing, or abstract quality:

A.1 *Betty* knows my *sister*. (names of persons)
A.2 *Chicago* is a large *city*. (names of places)
A.3 The *paper* blew out the *window*. (names of things)
A.4 *Gluttony* is a *vice*. (names of abstract qualities)

This definition attempts to state what a noun means. Looking at how a noun functions in a sentence is often more useful for purposes of classification:

A.5 The *typist* completed the *manuscript* and left it on my *desk*.

Typist functions as a subject, *manuscript* as a direct object, and *desk* as the object of a preposition. Although other structures such as pronouns, gerunds, and noun clauses may also serve in these functions, they are easily distinguished from nouns.

Several additional devices have been suggested for recognizing words as nouns:

1. They are frequently preceded by the articles *the, a,* and *an* or by demonstratives (*this, that, these, those*), possessives (*my, your, her,* etc.), numbers (*one, six, four,* etc.), or statements of quantity (*some, all, few,* etc.).

   A.6   *The reporter* saw *this gun* in *my hand.*

2. The noun and its modifiers may be replaced by a pronoun:

   A.7a   *The haughty woman* sat on *my ham sandwich.*
   b   *She* sat on *it.*

3. Many nouns have both singular and plural forms. The plural is usually spelled *-s* or *-es.*

Singular	Plural
duck	ducks
hat	hats
friend	friends
foot	feet
alumna	alumnae

   As the last two examples show, there are also a number of nouns that form their plurals by other means.

4. Some nouns are formed from other words by the addition of **derivational suffixes.** When such suffixes exist, they may be used to help classify a word as a noun.

Original Word	Derived Noun
assess (verb)	assess*ment*
play (verb)	play*er*
act (verb)	act*or*
confer (verb)	confer*ence*
repeat (verb)	repet*ition*
hostile (adjective)	hosti*lity*
careful (adjective)	careful*ness*
journal (noun)	journal*ism*
gang (noun)	gang*ster*

As you can see from the last two examples, the new word does not have to belong to a different part of speech from the original one.

Let us now look at a few examples that illustrate the devices for recognizing nouns:

A.8 I was sitting beside *Elizabeth Jacobs*.

Elizabeth Jacobs, the name of a person, functions as the object of a preposition. This is enough information for classifying the word as a noun.

A.9 Our *projections* proved overly optimistic.

It is not very helpful to say that *projections* is the name of a "thing." However, we can see that the word functions as the subject of *proved*, that it is modified by the possessive *our*, that it is a plural, and that it is derived from a verb by means of the suffix *-ion*. Furthermore, we can replace *our projections* with the pronoun *they*.

A.10 Bob ate a stale *sandwich*.

Sandwich functions as a direct object and is modified by the article *a*. It is also the name of a thing. If we need further proof, we can change the singular *a stale sandwich* to the plural *some stale sandwiches* or replace *sandwich* and its modifiers with *it*.

PRONOUNS

A **pronoun** is a word that replaces a noun and its modifiers.

A.11a *The fisherman* caught *a big fish*.
   b *He* caught *it*.

The pronouns *I*, *we*, and *you* do not replace nouns in the same sense as *he*, *she*, *it*, and *they* do. Also, such indefinite pronouns as *no one*, *something*, and *everybody* do not replace specific nouns.

It is doubtful that anyone ever uses this definition in recognizing pronouns since the list of pronouns is fairly small. In fact, the definition is more useful for classifying a word as a noun than for naming one as a pronoun. The following list gives most of the pronouns in English.

1. **Personal**

I	my, mine	me
you	your, yours	you
he	his	him
she	her, hers	her
it	its	it
we	our, ours	us
they	their, theirs	them

2. **Demonstrative:** *this, that, these, those* when no noun follows

   A.12   *That* is larger than *these* are.

3. **Indefinite**

$$\left.\begin{array}{l} \text{every} \\ \text{any} \\ \text{some} \\ \text{no} \end{array}\right\} + \left\{\begin{array}{l} \text{body} \\ \text{one} \\ \text{thing} \end{array}\right.$$

That is, *everybody, everyone, everything, anybody, anyone, anything*, and so on. All of these pronouns except *no one* are spelled as single words. Also included among the indefinite pronouns are such words as *all, any, some, much, both, either, neither*, and similar words naming quantities when there is no noun following.

   A.13   *Both* did *much* that was useful, but *neither* was aware of *anyone* in the room.

4. **Reflexive** and **Intensive**

myself	ourselves
yourself	yourselves
herself	themselves
himself	
itself	
oneself	

5. **Reciprocal**

> each other
> one another

6. **Interrogative:** *who, what, which, whose, whoever, whatever* when they ask questions

> **A.14**   *Who* are you?
> **A.15**   Do you know *what* that is?

7. **Relative:** *that, who, whom, whose* when they introduce adjective clauses

> **A.16**   The shoe *that* squeaked belonged to the man *who* left.

We easily recognize the italicized words in the following sentence as pronouns because we know that they always function as this part of speech:

> **A.17**   *He* told *everybody* about *himself*.

We do not ask whether they replace nouns or not.

VERBS

A **verb** expresses action, being, or state of being.

> **A.18**   The tiger *ran* through the trees. (action)
> **A.19**   We *are* your admirers. (being)
> **A.20**   Water *covered* the floor. (state of being)

State of being is often shortened to just *state* or *stative*. Two devices make useful supplements to the definition when you are classifying words as verbs:

1. A verb has tense. In sentences **A.18** and **A.20**, *ran* and *covered* are in the past tense, and *are* in **A.19** is in the present tense. If

you try to state the tense of any other words in these sentences, you immediately see that only verbs have tense.

2. Some verbs are formed by adding derivational suffixes or prefixes:

Original Word	Derived Verb
legal (adjective)	legal*ize*
light (adjective)	light*en*
orchestra (noun)	orchestr*ate*
beauty (noun)	beauti*fy*
courage (noun)	*en*courage

The element that has no suffix or prefix is called a **base**. A base such as *light* is called a **free base** because it can stand alone freely as a word. In addition to free bases, there are **bound bases,** which are never words by themselves but which serve as elements to which suffixes and prefixes are added. For example, the suffix -*ate* may be added to a large number of bound bases to provide such derived verbs as *operate, dedicate,* and *hesitate*.

Included among the verbs are the **auxiliary verbs** (also known as **helping verbs**). These consist of the **modals** (*can, could, may, might, shall, should, will, would, must*), and forms of *have, be,* and *do* when they precede other verbs:

Modals	Have	Be	Do
will sleep	*have* seen	*am* going	*does* write
could drop	*has* left	*was* knocking	*did* find

Have, be, and *do* may function as main verbs as well as auxiliaries:

A.21   We *have* eaten. (auxiliary)

A.22   We *have* a new car. (main verb)

The verb *be* is the most complex in the English language in that it has more forms than any other verb and is irregular in formation:

Present Tense	Past Tense	Participles	Infinitive
am	was	being	be
is	were	been	
are			

The combination of auxiliary (or auxiliaries) and main verb is called a **verb phrase.** The following are examples of verb phrases: *may read, has opened, are going, must have stopped, had been reading, will have been living*.

A few examples will show how we recognize verbs:

A.23   He always *slams* the door.

Slams is an action verb in the present tense.

A.24   They finally *realized* their error.

Realized expresses a state and is in the past tense. It also has the derivational suffix *-ize*.

A.25   They *have been screaming*.

Have, been, and *screaming* are all verbs, making the verb phrase *have been screaming. Have* and *been* are auxiliary verbs; the main verb *screaming* expresses action. The verb phrase is in the present perfect progressive tense (see Chapter 3).

A word may belong to one part of speech in one sentence and to a different part in another. *Care* provides an example:

A.26   They left the baby in our *care*.
A.27a We *care* for you.

In sentence **A.26**, *care* is a noun functioning as the object of the preposition *in;* it is modified by the possessive *our.* In sentence **A.27**, *care* is a verb in the present tense. It can easily be converted to past tense:

A.27b We *cared* for you.

It is often impossible to give the part of speech of a word in isolation, but once it is used in a sentence, we know how to classify it.

ADJECTIVES

An **adjective** modifies a noun or a pronoun. Its usual position is before the word it modifies or after a verb such as *be:*

A.28   *The tall* woman was *angry*.

The and *tall* are before *woman*. *Angry* also modifies *woman*, but it follows *was*, the past form of *be*. An adjective that comes before the word it modifies is called an **attributive adjective;** one that follows a verb and describes the subject is called a **predicate adjective.**
    There are several classes of adjectives:

1. A **descriptive adjective** gives a quality of the noun or pronoun.

    A.29   The *old* dog behind the *white* fence made a *horrible* noise.

2. An **article** is one of the words *a, an,* or *the.*

    A.30   *The* editor inserted *an* apostrophe.

3. A **demonstrative adjective** points out: *this, that, these, those.*

    A.31   *This* condominium costs more than *those* houses.

We call these words demonstrative adjectives because a noun follows each of them; if no noun follows, they are called demonstrative pronouns:

    A.32a   *That* car is mine, but *this* one is yours. (adjectives)
       b   *That* is mine, but *this* is yours. (pronouns)

4. A **numeral adjective** tells number.

    A.33a   *Two* people won *first* prize.

If we had omitted the word *people, two* would have been classified as a pronoun:

    A.33b   *Two* won first prize.

5. An **indefinite adjective** tells quantity and includes such words as *several, few, some, each, many, much, either,* and the like.

    A.34   A *few* people made *many* mistakes.

Like demonstratives and numerals, indefinites are classified as adjectives only if a noun follows them; otherwise, they are pronouns.

> **A.35a** *Several* people gave us *some* gifts. (adjectives)
>
> **b** *Several* gave us *some*. (pronouns)

Adjectives that are not descriptive (categories two through five) are sometimes called **limiting adjectives.**

Once you see that a given word modifies a noun or a pronoun, you usually need no further guides for classifying it as an adjective. When you need further help, you may consider the following devices:

1. The position between an article and a noun

> **A.36** The *old* shoes are under the *brown* chair.

2. Derivational suffixes

Original Word	Derived Adjective
care (noun)	care*ful*
marvel (noun)	marvel*ous*
conversation (noun)	conversation*al*
read (verb)	read*able*
differ (verb)	differ*ent*

As with the derivational suffixes for nouns and verbs, the listing is illustrative rather than exhaustive.

3. Comparison

Positive	Comparative	Superlative
old	old*er*	old*est*
rich	rich*er*	rich*est*
intricate	*more* intricate	*most* intricate
impulsive	*more* impulsive	*most* impulsive

Comparison does not distinguish an adjective from an adverb, but it shows that a given word does not belong to the other six parts of speech.

4. Modification by adverbs of degree such as *very, rather, extremely*

> **A.37** A *rather ugly* dog was following a *very handsome* man.

Adverbs may also be modified by these words, but the other parts of speech never are.

Using the definition of an adjective as a word that modifies a noun or pronoun, some elementary grammars classify possessives as adjectives:

my notebook   *Tom's* intelligence
our house   *the neighbors'* dog

Such a classification departs from that found in the grammars of other languages such as Latin, German, and Russian; it also departs from the treatment found in grammars of Old English and Middle English, as well as most scholarly grammars of Modern English. In all these works, possessives are called nouns or pronouns in the genitive case. Classifying these words as adjectives also leads to undesirable results:

> **A.38** My young brother's car is parked in the neighbors' drive.

If *brother's* and *neighbors'* are adjectives, then the words that modify them must be adverbs: *my, young,* and *the.* Also, in the following sentence the possessive *brother's* must be an adverb if it modifies the "adjective" *friend's:*

> **A.39** My brother's friend's car is outside.

On the other hand, if we call words like *brother's* and *friend's* possessive nouns, there is no mystery to their being modified by such unquestionable adjectives as *the, that, young,* and the like; we expect adjectives to modify nouns. Furthermore, since pronouns replace nouns, we are not surprised to find *his* replacing *my brother's:*

> **A.40a** *My brother's* friends are here.
>   **b** *His* friends are here.

In this book we follow the practice of scholarly grammars and classify possessives as nouns or pronouns.

We can now illustrate the devices for recognizing adjectives:

> **A.41**   We spent *an enjoyable* evening at home.

Enjoyable is an adjective because it modifies the noun *evening*. The position between the article *an* and the noun supports this classification, as does the derivational suffix *-able*. We could also insert the word *very* before it. Since *an* is always an adjective of the subclass article, we automatically know how to classify it even if we do not take the time to state that it modifies *evening*.

> **A.42**   Even the *weakest* students may have very *interesting* ideas.

The, an article, is always an adjective. *Weakest* modifies *students*. It is placed between an article and a noun and has the superlative ending *-est*. The adjective *interesting* modifies the noun *ideas* and is itself modified by *very*.

ADVERBS

An **adverb** modifies a verb, an adjective, another adverb, or an entire sentence.

> **A.43**   The door slammed *loudly*. (modifies the verb *slammed*)
> **A.44**   A *rather* ugly dog has been following me. (modifies the adjective *ugly*)
> **A.45**   She ate *very* slowly. (modifies the adverb *slowly*)
> **A.46**   *Certainly*, I am going with you. (modifies the entire sentence)

Adverbs may be classified according to meaning, depending upon whether they tell time, place, manner, and the like:

> **A.47**   I left home *yesterday*. (time)
> **A.48**   She lives *here*. (place)
> **A.49**   He hit me *hard*. (manner)

A.50 They were *extremely* rude. (degree)

A.51 We are *not* afraid. (negation)

Like adjectives, adverbs may be compared with *-er* and *-est* or with *more* and *most:*

A.52 I ran *fast*. (positive degree)

A.53 She ran *faster* than I did. (comparative degree)

A.54 You ran the *fastest* of all. (superlative degree)

Adverbs occasionally take the derivational suffixes *-wise* and *-ward:*

A.55 Turn it *clockwise*.

A.56 They rolled *backward*.

The most common adverbial suffix is *-ly*, used to form adverbs of manner and degree:

A.57 Betty opened the box *cautiously*. (manner)

A.58 She *rudely* interrupted the speaker. (manner)

A.59 They were *extremely* polite. (degree)

This suffix should be used with caution, since it occurs on adjectives as well as adverbs. When *-ly* is added to an adjective, the result is an adverb:

A.60 The engineer started the motor *carefully*.

However, when *-ly* is added to a noun, the new word is usually an adjective:

A.61 The *friendly* man opened the door.

The best test for the part of speech of a word ending in the suffix *-ly* is to see what it modifies. If it modifies a verb, such as *started* in **A.60**, it is an adverb. If it modifies a noun, as *man* in **A.61**, it is an adjective. A word such as *daily* may be either an adjective or an adverb, depending on what it modifies:

A.62 They swim *daily*. (adverb)

A.63 That was a *daily* occurrence. (adjective)

Daily in **A.62** is an adverb modifying the verb *swim*, but in **A.63** it is an adjective modifying *occurrence*.

The following sentence illustrates the use of adverbs:

> **A.64** We drove *quite rapidly* on the hilly road *yesterday*.

Rapidly, an adverb of manner, modifies the verb *drove*. It is modified by the adverb of degree *quite* and has the derivational suffix *-ly*. *Quite* is an adverb of degree, and it modifies *rapidly*. *Yesterday*, an adverb of time, modifies *drove*. *Rapidly* and *yesterday* tell how and when we drove; *quite* tells how rapidly we drove. *Hilly* is not an adverb but an adjective modifying *road;* the *-ly* suffix was added to the noun *hill*.

PREPOSITIONS

A **preposition** is a word that shows the relationship between its object and another word in the sentence. Although this definition is vague, no better one has been provided. Most people learn to recognize prepositions by examining sentences in which they occur. A preposition introduces a prepositional phrase (italicized in the examples):

> **A.65** A man *with a cold* sat *in the park*.

A prepositional phrase consists of a preposition, its object, and any modifiers of the object. *Cold* and *park* are the objects of the prepositions in **A.65**. Notice that the normal position for a preposition is *before* its object, as the prefix *pre-* suggests. Here are some more examples:

> **A.66** Someone *at the dance* stepped *on my foot*.
>
> **A.67** No one *but Sam* would sit *between you and me*.

Notice that *but* is a preposition when it means "except."

A prepositional phrase usually modifies a noun, a pronoun, or a verb. In **A.66,** *at the dance* modifies *someone;* in **A.67,** *but Sam* modifies *no one*. Adverbial uses can be seen also in these sentences. In **A.66,** *on my foot* modifies *stepped*, and in **A.67,** *between you and me* modifies *would sit*. Do not call *on* or *between* adverbs. It is the entire phrase that modifies the verb, not *on* or *between* by itself. *On* and *between* are prepositions.

Some prepositions were originally two or more words. Such words as *into* and *throughout* are spelled solid and are so common that you are usually unaware that they were ever two words. There are others that are spelled separately but which should be considered as single prepositions, called **phrasal prepositions:**

> **A.68** We ran inside *because of* the rain.
>
> **A.69** *Except for* the silly games, we enjoyed the party.

When a noun is part of the structure, there is less agreement on classification:

> **A.70** I stood *in back of Judy*.
>
> **A.71** We came here *by way of Elm Avenue*.
>
> **A.72** He stood *under a tree in our back yard*.

It is possible to analyze all of these as combinations of two prepositional phrases, with the second modifying the object of the first phrase. This seems to be the only reasonable analysis for **A.72,** where *in our back yard* tells which tree; also, there is no single word that could substitute for *under a tree in*. The structures in **A.70** and **A.71,** however, could be classified as single prepositional phrases. With this interpretation, *in back of* would be a phrasal preposition synonymous with *behind*, and *by way of* would be treated like *via*.

Below are the most commonly used prepositions:

aboard	beyond	other than
about	but	out
above	by	out of
according to	concerning	outside
across	despite	over
after	down	past
against	due to	pending
ahead of	during	regarding
along with	except	since
among	except for	together with
apart from	for	through
around	from	throughout
as	in	till
as for	including	to
at	inside	toward
away from	inside of	under

barring	into	underneath
because of	like	until
before	near	up
behind	next to	upon
below	notwithstanding	versus
beneath	of	via
beside	off	with
besides	on	within
between	onto	without

Some of these words may function as other parts of speech as well as prepositions. When *since, after,* and *before* introduce adverb clauses, they are subordinate conjunctions. Others may be adverbs:

> **A.73**   The spider ran *up* the wall. (preposition)
> **A.74**   The teacher looked *up*. (adverb)

Remember that prepositions introduce phrases containing objects. *Up* in the first sentence qualifies as a preposition because it introduces the phrase *up the wall*. But *up* in **A.74** cannot be a preposition because it does not have an object.

CONJUNCTIONS

A **conjunction** joins words, phrases, or clauses. If it is a **coordinating conjunction,** it joins the same kinds of items (*e.g.,* two or more adjectives or two or more prepositional phrases). The most common coordinating conjunctions are *and, or, nor, but, yet, for,* and *so:*

> **A.75**   Sticks *and* stones may break my bones, *but* words will never harm me. (In this example, *and* joins two nouns; *but* joins two clauses.)

Correlative conjunctions, a subclass of coordinating conjunctions, come in pairs: *both . . . and, not only . . . but also, either . . . or, neither . . . nor:*

> **A.76**   You are *not only* intelligent *but also* polite.

Subordinating conjunctions, the other class, introduce dependent clauses:

> **A.77** *If* you lose your way, consult this map.
>
> **A.78** I know *that* you are intelligent.

INTERJECTIONS

An **interjection** is a word that expresses emotion and has no grammatical function in the sentence:

> **A.79** *Oh*, I see what you mean.
>
> **A.80** *Fiddlesticks!*

As these two examples show, the emotion may be slight or strong.

CONCLUSION

The parts of speech of some words are so obvious that you are able to mark them without much effort:

> **A.81** Michael is with us.

These words could hardly be anything other than noun, verb, preposition, and pronoun, in that order. Most sentences contain at least some words that are very easy to classify.

For other words, you need to observe the devices you have learned in this chapter. These devices are essential when a word may be used as more than one part of speech.

> **A.82** Martha will *light* the fire. (verb)
>
> **A.83** The *light* bothers me. (noun)

With a change in meaning, *light* can also be an adjective:

> **A.84** You should wear *light* colors.

There are many such words, and their number is growing, as you have probably noticed with the shift of *fun* from noun to adjective in *a fun time* or the use of *party* as a verb in *We partied all night*.

During the 1940s and 1950s, linguists used nonsense words to show that many words can be classified as to part of speech even if their meanings are not known.

A.85   A wattal flump has zackized our shrotement in the breations.

Classification is possible because of suffixes, word order, and such known words as articles, auxiliaries, and prepositions. We decide that *wattal* is an adjective because of the suffix *-al* and its position between an article and a noun. We call *flump* a noun because it is modified by the article *a* and because it is a subject. *A wattal flump* seems to be like *a comical monkey. Zackized* almost has to be a verb with the derivational suffix *-ize* and the ending *-ed*, which is compatible with the auxiliary *has*. We know that *our*, unlike *ours*, must have a noun after it, and *shrotement*, with the suffix *-ment*, is the most likely candidate, especially since *in the breations* is clearly a prepositional phrase. Finally, we have a number of ways of knowing that *breations* is a noun. The article *the* always has a noun after it. Second, *breations* is the only word that could be the object of the preposition *in*. It also has a plural ending and the derivational suffix *-ion*. When you are dealing with nonsense words, remember that some of these devices are more valid than others. The use of prepositions and articles holds whether the "noun" is a known word or not. However, you cannot be certain that an ending such as *-ion* is actually a derivational suffix. Look at the words *promotion* and *lotion*, for example. If you did not already know that there is a verb *promote* but not **lot*, you would not be able to say that *-ion* is a suffix in *promotion* but not in *lotion*. You do not have this information about nonsense words. Nevertheless, when used with caution, nonsense words provide good illustrations of the various devices for recognizing parts of speech.

As the examples show, there is no single device that can be used exclusively in classifying words as to part of speech. If you understand how to use all the devices presented in this chapter, including the traditional definitions, you can select the most useful means in each sentence.

EXERCISES

A.   Underline each word with a derivational suffix and name its part of speech.

   1.   They surely realize the suddenness of your action.

   2.   Her persuasive arguments will frighten the lethargic workers.

3. An Italian hypnotized the foolish waitress.
4. His refusal was not a personal rejection of Marxism.
5. The contemptible resident activated the machinery.

B. Give the part of speech of each word.

1. Kevin cautioned us about the heat.
2. We heat the old shed with caution.
3. Those cautious hunters darkened the cabin early.
4. Everyone emerged cautiously from the building after dark.
5. Many are building new carports.
6. Many members renewed their cards.
7. The speaker began with a humorous anecdote.
8. These accomplishments will motivate her.
9. These are not level.
10. I will level with you now.
11. The salesperson seemed on the level.
12. Bobby had a talk with the typist.
13. He talked and typed at the same time.
14. The doctor went inside the office.
15. Six worried patients waited inside.
16. The stores are upping their prices again.
17. The new lodger's room is on the second floor.
18. Your rude remarks really floored us.
19. The gapist's coopment pledened me chippily.
20. Some tattous bergsters were crimpting medwise under the goopie.

Index

Absolute phrase, 142–43, 157
Accusative case, 186
Active voice, 62
Adjective, 67–68, 86–89, 146, 148,
   223–27
Adverb, 13–15, 227–29
Adverb clause, 140–42, 157
Adverbial, 41, 105, 139–40, 143–
   45, 150–51
Adverbial complement, 33–36
Adverbial noun, 14–15, 65
Antecedent, 177–82, 183
Appositive, 30, 119–21, 145, 147,
   166, 188–89, 190
Article, 79
Auxiliary, 63–64

Case, 186–93
Cognate object, 12
Commas, 108–9, 120, 142, 163–64
Common noun, 78
Complement, 25
Complex sentence, 159
Compound, 89–91
Compound-complex sentence, 159
Compound sentence, 158
Compound structure, 156–75
Conjunction, 117, 141, 159–62,
   231–32
Conjunctive adverb, 162
Coordinate adjectives, 88
Coordinating conjunction, 159–
   61, 165, 231
Copulative verb, 25
Correlative conjunction, 161

Dangling modifier, 146
Definite article, 79
Delayed object, 119
Delayed subject, 119
Deletion, 66, 127, 130–31
Demonstrative, 79, 88–89, 94
Determiner, 89
Direct object, 8–13, 19–20, 104,
   118, 121, 126, 130, 188

Elliptical clause, 110
Embedded sentence, 205–6, 211
Expletive, 8, 118, 209
Extraposition, 118, 130, 146–48,
   209

Faulty parallelism, 166–67
Future tense, 46–48

Gerund phrase, 124–129, 157, 178,
   184
Get passive, 68–71

Historical present, 45–46

Imperative mood, 53–54
Indefinite article, 79
Indefinite pronoun, 65–66, 128,
   180–81, 220
Indicative mood, 53
Indirect object, 18–21, 121, 126,
   188

Infinitive phrase, 129–31, 143–45, 157, 178, 184–85
Inflected possessive, 84
Intensive pronoun, 182–83, 220
Interjection, 232
Interrogative pronoun, 221
Intransitive verb, 11
Irregular verb, 42, 50

Linking verb, 25, 68

Modals, 54
Mood, 53–56

Nominative case, 186–87
Nonrestrictive modifier, 105–11
Noun, 78, 128, 217–19
Noun clause, 117–24, 157, 206
Noun phrase, 77–93, 177

Objective case, 186–87
Objective complement, 31–33, 104, 121, 126
Object of a preposition, 77, 121, 122, 126, 188, 229

Parallel structure, 166–67
Participle, 100–5, 109, 145, 147–48, 157, 178, 184
Particle, 16
Passive, 61–76, 102–3
Past participle, 50, 62, 67–68, 101–3, 145, 147
Past tense, 41–44
Perfect progressive tenses, 51–53
Perfect tenses, 49–51
Periphrastic possessive, 84
Possessive, 81–86, 94, 125, 186–87
Predicate, 4–6
Predicate adjective, 25, 27–29, 104, 127

Predicate nominative, 25, 192–93
Predicate noun, 25–27, 64, 77, 118, 121, 126, 130
Preposition, 15–18, 98–99, 105, 229–31
Present participle, 48, 101–3, 129, 145, 147
Present tense, 44–46
Progressive tenses, 48–49
Pronoun, 176–200, 219–21
Proper noun, 78
Pseudo-intransitive verb, 12

Questions, 36–37

Reflexive pronoun, 69, 183–86, 220
Regular verb, 42, 50
Relative adverb, 99–100
Relative clause, 97–100, 120–21, 157, 205
Relative pronoun, 96–99, 120
Restrictive modifier, 105–11

Semicolon, 158, 164
Shall and *will*, 47–48
Simple sentence, 158
Subject, 3–4, 77, 117, 121, 126, 127, 130, 188
Subjective complement, 24–25
Subject-verb agreement, 5–6, 169–71
Subjunctive mood, 54–56, 193
Subordinating conjunction, 141, 231–32
Subordination, 96
SVO order, 10–11, 61, 116, 203–5

Tense, 41–53
Third person, 44
Transitive verb, 11

Verb, 5–6, 221–23
Verb-particle combination, 16–18
Verb phrase, 40–60

Who and *whom*, 122–23, 191–92
Will and *shall*, 47–48